STEPBYSTEP

Resources for Changing Lives

A series published in cooperation with
THE CHRISTIAN COUNSELING AND EDUCATIONAL FOUNDATION,
Glenside, Pennsylvania

Susan Lutz, Series Editor

Available in the series:

STEP**BY**STEP

DIVINE GUIDANCE FOR ORDINARY CHRISTIANS

JAMES C. PETTY

PUBLISHING
P.O. BOX 817 • PHILLIPSBURG • NEW JERSEY 08865-0817

Printed in the United States of America
Composition by Colophon Typesetting

Library of Congress Cataloging-in-Publication Data

Petty, James C., 1944–
    Step by step : divine guidance for ordinary Christians / James C. Petty.
        p.   cm. — (Resources for changing lives)
    Includes bibliographical references.
    ISBN 0-87552-603-9
    1. Spiritual life—Christianity. 2. God—Will.   I. Title.
II. Series.
BV4501.2.P432   1999
248.4—dc21   99-31303

To Dr. Cornelius Van Til,

who pointed me to fear the Lord

as the beginning of wisdom

CONTENTS

Contents

**Part Four: Seeking Guidance: The Seven Elements
of Biblical Decision Making**

PREFACE

"WHAT is the will of God for my life?"

If you had asked Christ that question when he was here on earth, what would he have said? He would have answered, "Love God and then love others as I have loved you" (see John 15:1–17). Paul the apostle answers the question in a different way in 1 Thessalonians 4:3: "This is the will of God, even your sanctification" (KJV). The point is that, at one level, it does not take a lot of discernment to know the will of God for your life.

Yet currently there are about thirty-five evangelical books in print on this topic (this one makes thirty-six) because we all struggle to know how those profound statements apply *practically* to our everyday decisions. How do we know the will of God for entering into marriage? For educational and vocational decisions? For guidance in conflict, family, and ministry situations? (For example, should I presume to write a book on guidance?)

Most of us will make five to ten of these life-shaping decisions in our lifetimes. Beyond that, we make dozens of smaller ones every day. Shall I stop writing and eat lunch—to avoid becoming grumpy? How shall I begin this book so that folks will want to read it? Shall I buy lunch or make it from the bounty of the fridge—saving lots of money?

The difficulty of knowing when and how to make connections between the great commandments and these kinds of decisions have led many to give up trying. Instead, they seek some other way to know the will of God. They suggest looking for signs, "fleece," "open doors," promptings, peaceful sensations, audible voices, or perhaps even inaudible ones. Others suggest looking to spiritual directors, disciplers, church elders, prophecy, or "words of knowledge." From one angle, such approaches seems rather tame compared to the extraordinary and sometimes bizarre ways (casting lots, Balaam's donkey) God revealed himself to people in the Bible. Which way is right?

Just yesterday a friend and I were talking about this writing project. The first thing he wanted to know was what I thought about Christians who claimed to hear the audible voice of God offering them guidance. Evidently a famous missionary was quoted as hearing such a voice, and he based his calling to missionary service upon it. My friend, a committed Christian, wondered if he should ask for that kind of direction in his life. To date, God had never addressed him that way.

Millions of Christians are asking that question in one form or another. They agree with Jesus, "I have come to do your will, O God," but are not sure what that will is, much less how to discover it. That is why I have written this book. It will not reveal what God's will is for you in specific situations, but it will help you to understand how to pursue it in godly and fruitful ways.

But before any of us approaches the topic of how to know the will of God, we must answer this question: "Why do we want to know it?" What is our purpose in seeking guidance from God, and what is God's purpose in providing it? God does not offer wisdom from above in order to help us secure success on earth. Some success may be a by-product under certain conditions, but it should not be our goal. If God (and his guidance) is just a means to some other goal, we are (consciously or unconsciously) using God. In that case, the goal we seek functions as our "god" and competes with the true God for our allegiance and trust. No matter how good the goal is (family, ministry, marriage, education, or job), James 4:4 calls it "friendship with the world" and equates it with "hatred of God." But if your motive is to glorify, enjoy, and serve God, he says, "I will instruct you and teach you in the way you should go; I will counsel you and watch over you" (Ps. 32:8).

With that said, it is the purpose of *Step by Step* to systematically examine what the Bible says about knowing the will of God. I hope we will be encouraged to discover that godly saints through the years have identified and tested a foundation of powerful theological truths that can guide our way. The biblical doctrines of providence, revelation, inspiration, and illumination carry within them the answers our theologically unaware generation needs. Saints since the early church have longed to know and do the will of God. They asked questions of Scripture and sought answers there. That, very simply, is what theology is, and that is what we shall attempt to do with the subject of discerning the will of God.

We will be looking at both biblical and contemporary examples of guidance, but our primary focus will be on what is actually taught in Scripture about the subject. In Parts One, Two, and Three we will look at the theology of guidance. Part Four is a case study, showing you how to apply the principles to a real life situation. This case study embodies many of the most pressing questions on guidance that I encounter as a counselor.

The appendix contains exercises and material relevant to guidance questions about time management and priorities.

As I've said, this book cannot provide specific answers for your guidance decisions. I believe that guidance comes when you learn to apply the Word of God to your life in the wisdom provided by the Holy Spirit. However, I hope that this book will encourage and practically direct you to the fountain and source of all wisdom and guidance, Jesus Christ (Col. 2:2). It is also meant to answer questions you may have about the process of guidance, thereby increasing your confidence in God to provide it.

As I have wrestled with these questions, I am reminded of the limitations of our minds to truly comprehend the relation of the infinite God to the finite creation. When seeking to understand guidance theologically, we bump into that limitation often. For example, what is the relationship between human free will and God's control? I hope we are not so foolish as to insist on totally comprehending that relationship and others like it—especially as we begin to appreciate the majesty of the true God and his management of the cosmos.

I mention this because when it comes to guidance, there is a strong temptation to look so hard for a consistent biblical formula that we ignore Scripture passages that do not fit into our views. That, of course, is a subtle form of intellectual idolatry. Someone once said, "God made man in his image, and we returned the favor." May God deliver us from that practice.

Instead, I pray that we may humble ourselves and prove teachable as we handle God's Word, particularly in this difficult and controversial area. May God protect us from the seductive trap of twisting or ignoring any part of Scripture to bolster an outcome that supports our views.

Rather, I hope we will gain a sense of wonder at what God has done in giving us such a vital, inexhaustible revelation of himself. The Word of God is more than equal to the challenges of the twenty-first century! It sheds a brightening light into the church, equipping God's people to be salt and light in a changing world. I pray that this will continue to be the case as the church sits at the feet of Christ to learn more clearly the theology of guidance and the practice of a Spirit-led life.

ACKNOWLEDGMENTS

AT several points in this book, I question a specific view or identify it as erroneous. In most cases I have chosen not to list proponents of the view, for the sake of charity and Christian unity. An earlier form of this work was submitted to Westminster Theological Seminary for the Doctor of Ministry Degree. It contains a complete annotated bibliography for those interested in more information on the views held by various writers. In cases where there is sufficient reason to deal more extensively (and therefore more fairly) with a divergent view, or where I have needed to quote a passage, I have named the author. These authors are professing Christians with a high view of Scripture. I gladly acknowledge them as my brothers and sisters in Christ despite any differences of approach. I confess that I have much to learn from all of them.

I want to thank Ed Welch and Susan Lutz, my colleagues at the Christian Counseling and Educational Foundation. Their encouragement and suggestions, and Sue's extensive editing, have been critical to the successful completion of this book.

I am deeply grateful to God for Marsha Petty, my wife; for her encouragement, companionship, and cheerful help with reading this work in various forms during the last two years.

Acknowledgments

I would also like to acknowledge the influence of many former parishioners, family members, and current students who have encouraged me to write down these thoughts.

PART ONE   *The Promise of Guidance*

CHAPTER 1

DOES GOD GUIDE US?

A clear and vivid thought entered my head. "Slow down! Let the boy on the path behind you catch up; then tell him about Christ." I was an eighth grader walking on my well-worn path home from school when that distinct thought captured my mind. For about a hundred yards I tried to resist the idea but was, of course, afflicted with guilt. Finally, I knelt down and pretended to retie my Keds tennis shoes (circa 1956). The boy caught up to me. I don't remember what I said to him, but somehow, fifteen minutes later he was praying to receive Christ.

That was the first time I thought I had received guidance from God. Boy, was I relieved! At last I had some concrete evidence that God knew who I was. As an added bonus, I had fulfilled my obligation to "witness" and even had an evangelistic notch in my belt. I quietly took comfort in that incident during my spiritually bleak high school career. And I waited for God to "speak" again. After all, I thought, a word from God every five or six years seemed like a reasonable minimum for any kind of meaningful relationship.

Were my expectations too high? Were they too low? Was I, in fact, missing God's efforts to communicate with me? I didn't know. And I suspect that many Christians have wrestled with such questions.

Does the God of the Bible, in fact, reach down and specifically, personally direct us? Does he communicate direction and information to us that we would not otherwise know? And if he does, how does he do it? How can I enjoy the benefit of such direction? These are the questions we will seek to answer in this book.

Library or Airplane Cockpit?

We will be looking for our answers in the pages of the Bible, but not because I view these as abstract theological questions. The answers we find will profoundly affect the real life choices we make. When we seek guidance from God, we are not like a student pondering the great questions of life safely seated in a library carrel. We are more like a pilot seeking to land a commercial airliner filled with passengers. For a pilot, even the best of them, the pressing need is for current information on position, weather, visibility, and local air traffic. The thought that communication with the control tower might not be possible, predictable, and clear is more than unsettling—it is the stuff of horror films.

In a sense, all of us are like pilots in flight. The decisions we make will affect many others, and many things can go wrong. Our relationships, our jobs, our health and safety can be compromised by a single bad decision.

It is amazing to stop and think about the life-changing consequences of certain decisions. For example, we make decisions in early childhood about how to cope with the bully down the street. Those decisions then become patterns that affect the way we handle conflict today.

For the unmarried, the decision to seek a second date with a member of the opposite sex can be among the most important decisions in life. Whether or not to seek medical advice regarding a pesky rash could be a life-or-death decision.

Should you confront your boss with what you believe is an error or moral breach on his part? If you do, you will either be a hero or a new face in the unemployment line. Should you bring up your suspicions of your son's homosexuality? With that kind of question, it is impossible to "get the toothpaste back in the tube" once it is out.

Should you replace a worn tire now with money you don't have (using a credit card) or save up and buy it with cash? You could either look like a budgeting whiz or wind up dead when your car skids on a wet street. Pursuing a new, out-of-town job opportunity could turn out to be the key to your career or a stressful disaster that leaves you depressed and bankrupt.

If communication from God on these kinds of issues is available, we do not want to be tuned to the wrong channel! Nor do we want to be unaware that such communication is even possible. Life offers us abundant opportunities for crash landings and precious few years, and so it is not surprising that Christians have always addressed the issue of divine guidance with great energy.

However, until the industrialized age, most Christian writings on guidance emphasized guidance *to* God, not guidance *from* God. Writers such as John of the Cross (1542–91), Bernard of Clairvaux (1090–1153), Francois Fenelon (1651–1715), Richard Rolle (1290–1349), and a host of others provided direction on how to experience God's presence and character.

In those days many of the pressing problems of guidance (Whom should I marry? What should I do with my life?) did not have much prominence. Marriages were largely arranged by family and community. Job opportunities were usually related to the occupation of one's parents. Hope of significant upward mobility was considered the stuff of dreams—not the way of the real world. The biggest decision for the Christian probably revolved around whether or not to join a spiritual order (and a monastery or nunnery) to seek God "full time" or to remain on the outside and support those who were vocationally "religious."

I believe that today's lack of interest in guidance to God has resulted in a lot more questions about how to seek guidance from God. We simply don't know God as well as previous generations of believers did and, as we shall see, guidance from God is rooted in our knowledge of him. The more one knows of God's character and desires, the better one can live to be conformed to the image of Christ—and make the many daily decisions that must be made.

A Decision a Minute

And how the pace of decision making has changed—at least in the industrial and postindustrial West! Now there are decisions to be made minute by minute. For example, a married couple today must answer, in a few short years, questions that most Christians in the 1600s did not even have to ask. Here is a sample list:

➤ How many children should we have?

➤ When should we have those children?

➤ Should we bottle-feed that baby?

➤ Should we adopt?

➤ Should both partners leave the home and enter the work force?

➤ Should I divorce or adjust to the evils of my spouse?

➤ Should we use a public, private, or Christian school?

➤ How hard should we push our child in music, sports, computers?

➤ Which church or youth group should we choose?

➤ How many lifestyle "risk factors" are acceptable?

➤ Should we change careers?

➤ How much should we invest in a child's higher education?

➤ How much debt should we incur for school, home, or car?

➤ What back-up plans should we have for potential job loss?

➤ How much auto, liability, and hospitalization insurance should we carry?

➤ How much should we set aside now for retirement?

➤ How should we invest those retirement funds?

All these decisions and dozens more are made within a space of ten to twelve years after marriage. And many of these decisions are remade almost daily. Along with these, of course, are all the decisions about balancing the priorities these issues reflect. The increasing pace of change only increases the frequency of such required decision making.

Changes in the World of Work

The rising number of decisions is not something encountered only in marriage and the home. It happens too in the world of work. The labor market is undergoing dramatic structural change because of the transition from the postwar industrial boom to the information age of global competition. Entire industries (steel, textiles, electronics, etc.) have moved to developing nations with twelve million jobs lost in American manufacturing communities.

Though most of these jobs were with large companies, global competition is no longer something that only confronts Ford Motor Company. With the Internet, you can search the entire world for the best price on a CD recording, a brand of shoe, or an electric drill—and all in less time than it takes to use the yellow pages. Few businesses are safe from the competition and change that this information explosion brings. In the midst of this change we long for guidance from God in situations that seem outside our control.

Chapter One

The Empty Wallet

Connected to the changing world of work are tectonic shifts in distribution of income. Employed Americans fear substantial loss of earning power as they face the prospect of a shrinking middle class. *The Economist* magazine reports a University of Michigan study that tracked the same families since 1968. The study found that 65 percent of white American men who turned twenty-one before 1980 had reached the middle class by age thirty. Yet only 47 percent who turned twenty-one after 1980 achieved middle class by age thirty. For black males the comparable statistics were 29 percent and 19 percent respectively (*The Economist,* February 24, 1996, 30).

This same article reported a study by New York University economist Edward Wolff, who found that in 1979 America's richest 1 percent held 21 percent of our national wealth. By 1992 the top 1 percent held 42 percent of the assets. While Wolff did not include the value of pensions and benefits (which would moderate the statistics), the trend is striking. Although the U.S. economic pie is growing, there is going to be less of it for the middle class to divide. Statistics for the poor are even more dramatic.

This sense of uneasiness is illustrated daily in the lives of those seeking to re-enter the work force after being "downsized" (laid off). The average American worker re-entering the work force today takes a 20 percent pay cut (*The Economist,* February 24, 1996, 31). Those who are keeping up are those who have developed the specialized skills needed in the information age. Those skills are developed through education but, unfortunately, educational costs have risen at a rate much higher than the rate of inflation. This forces prospective students to weigh the value of education against the economic consequences of graduation with substantial debt.

For all these reasons we have enormous numbers of people experiencing crisis or ongoing anxiety about their work. Large numbers quite properly seek guidance from friends, family, and professionals. Yet, it seems, sometimes we seek a road map through a world that is changing so quickly that the maps have not yet been printed.

Knowing the Right Hand from the Left

There is an even greater sense in which our society suffers a lack of guidance. It was said of Sodom that morally the citizens could not tell their right hands from their left. While we may have a way to go to compete with Sodom and Gomorrah, the parallel is appropriate: values obvious to previous generations within the Judeo-Christian world have little acceptance among today's cultural gatekeepers. Instead, there is an almost total individualism that seeks first its own personal peace and affluence (to use Francis Schaeffer's phrase).

Today's college freshmen are normally given a briefing (in the name of tolerance) about how to determine whether one is heterosexual, bisexual, or homosexual. They are told that "sexual orientation" is a personal, nonmoral issue. Instead of a required course in ethics or religion, many colleges today require a course in "pluralism," which is really a course in relativism. It undermines any notion of absolute values that might be morally binding on all. Instead, morals are viewed simply as one's personal psychological reactions to outside situations. Guilt is only psychological, as is moral rightness.

To be sure, there is still behavioral and emotional momentum from our Christian past. But the powerful words of a bygone Christian ethic (justice, love, tolerance, liberty, oppression, peace, and liberation) are now usurped to provide emotional force for the propaganda of groups as pagan as the American Nazi Party and Queer Nation and as everyday as television advertising. The concepts are stripped of any Godward reference and true moral force. Instead, they are used as weapons to promote an agenda. Consequently, our young people cannot rely on our society's corporate wisdom for boundaries and direction. There really isn't any.

What remains is only the momentum of the Christian past. Our culture is like a great ocean liner of the nineteenth century sailing confidently toward the lighthouse in the harbor, only to encounter a dense fog bank. The captain knows the general direction in which to head but is unable to fix or correct his course. The longer he sails under zero visibility, the greater the combined error caused by wind, tide, and currents.

The people of the nineteenth century were just as sinful as we are today, but they tended to have moral categories to remind them of that fact. Twentieth-century morals have no condemning or justifying power at all; they do not really even qualify as morals. Today we are engulfed in a fog bank of blindness that few nineteenth-century folks (except the intellectual elite) experienced.

Our culture therefore cannot understand the divinely instituted moral bond that undergirds the family, marriage, civic community, and the workplace. These relationships and structures are portrayed as products of our biological and social evolution. They are merely means for achieving individual personal goals, with no intrinsic value or transcendent validity. This blindness is demonstrated in our high rate of divorce and incarceration, increased domestic violence, and the growing confusion about the institution of marriage and the family.

If guidance comes from wisdom and wisdom is the application of values to life, then our culture—despite its great technological knowledge—cannot provide real guidance. Our society can only offer instruction in cleverness, self-interest, self-esteem, and ways to gain power for the self. Self-help motivational books like *Think and Grow Rich* (Hill 1960) are classics of our age just because they reflect, in rather crass terms, the guiding wisdom of our time.

To Meet the Need

Against this background, God's reputation for providing guidance to his people corporately and personally has a particular appeal. The hope of divine guidance strikes a deep chord in the soul of the Christian as well as in many confused and directionless non-Christians. A true and living God who knows the beginning from the end, a God who is willing to guide those who will follow, looks as good to us as he did to David, King of Israel. David sang,

> *If I rise on the wings of the dawn,*
> *if I settle on the far side of the sea,*
> *even there your hand will guide me. (Ps. 139:9–10)*

Such a promise offers new opportunities for the Christian church to witness to a culture where the American dream has died and no one knows another way.

The need for guidance has been aggressively addressed in popular Christian books. Pastors frequently address guidance issues in their sermons. Conferences such as InterVarsity's Urbana Missions Convention are built around guidance. Pastoral counselors are often involved in directing the lives of many Christians.[1]

And while it is encouraging to see such a response from today's Christian leaders, it leaves us with a rather profound problem: At the very time when the need for guidance is most obvious, these writers and teachers often contradict each other at key points. To make matters more difficult (with the exception of two or three authors), they

---

1 In preparation for writing this book, I reviewed some thirty-five Christian books on the subject of divine guidance. An annotated bibliography is available on these books as part of the version of this work submitted for my D.Min. degree at Westminster Theological Seminary, Glenside, Pennsylvania.

address their issues in a nontheological way. That is, their books offer no serious study of Scripture, no in-depth interaction with larger theological principles. We are given stories, illustrations, and references to Scripture, but little or no critical theological reflection. The books usually give the writer's conclusion—period.

There is a place for that kind of pastoral direction, assuming that the deep study of Scripture has taken place. However, it is my concern that such study has not happened, or if it has, it is not presented to the readers. It is ironic that the authors of books on guidance don't seem to be guided themselves to a common methodology or understanding.

Christian theologians have continued to address issues of medical ethics, church and state, inerrancy, charismatic phenomena, and world poverty, but have not yet done much on the issue of guidance, an issue that affects so many Christians. The friend who asked me about the validity of guidance through the audible voice of God really wanted to know. He wondered if he needed more faith to pursue real guidance, as opposed to just using his God-given brain. If God is speaking, the stakes are very high that we listen. Yet confusion reigns about what the Bible teaches. This volume attempts to address that problem.

My goal is to help you understand the issues of guidance from a systematically biblical perspective. You will then be able to decide prayerfully what God has said about seeking to know his will. Through this study I hope that you can come to a confident decision about how to seek guidance from God. I hope to give you the confidence to say, "Surely goodness and mercy shall follow me all the days of my life."

For Review and Reflection

1. Have you had one or more experiences that you would consider divine guidance? Describe them.

2. Were there any biblical passages that came to mind to help you understand the experience(s)?

3. Were you taught that guidance comes by God revealing part or all of his specific plan for our lives?

4. What Scriptures did you associate with that teaching?

5. Have you ever sought divine guidance? What was the outcome?

CHAPTER 2

HOW DOES
GOD GUIDE US?
THREE VIEWS

AMONG biblically committed Christians, there are three main schools of thought about how God guides.[1] Reviewing these three basic positions will help us as we begin our discussion.

The Traditional View

The most popular view among biblically committed Christians is what Garry Friesen calls the "Traditional View" (Friesen 1980, 22–77). While not really "traditional" (since the view only became popular in the twentieth century), it certainly is now the majority view. This perspective holds that God has a specific and detailed plan for each Christian's life. Guidance involves discerning that plan. Since this spe-

---

1 There is an additional view, which I will call the "priestly view." This view emphasizes that we find guidance from God by looking to those whom God has appointed over us. There is great variety in the way this idea is worked out among different groups. In Roman Catholic circles, it often involves the services of a "spir-

cific individual plan is not recorded in the Bible and cannot be deduced from it, each Christian must (it is said) discern it by other means. God is believed to be ready to reveal this plan, step by step, to those who ask him to do so.

This first perspective teaches that God's plan can be discerned by looking carefully into a combination of circumstances, spiritual promptings, inner voices, personal peace of mind, and the counsel of others. The evangelical writers who hold this view are quick to point out that guidance always comes within the bounds of general biblical commandments and in response to prayer. A Christian would never be led by God to do something the Bible calls sin. Biblical prohibitions form the outer boundary within which these other vehicles of guidance can function.

This passage from J. Oswald Sanders is typical of writers in this vein.

> Does God have an ideal and detailed will and plan for every life? Is this a valid concept or is it only a view that has been read into Scripture wrongly? If there is such a plan, it is of paramount importance that we get to know it. (Sanders 1992, 10)

Sanders believes that such a plan exists and that therefore we should seek to understand it. He and others make a case for such an "ideal and detailed plan" by appealing to the sovereignty of God. No one would disagree with that fact, but these writers insert a hidden

---

itual director" who controls the spiritual growth of the disciple. In the 1970s the "Shepherding Movement" flashed across the U.S., teaching that most important decisions should be approved by one's elders or pastor. They functioned as providers of God's direction on all important subjects. This emphasis is not currently exerting much force in the U.S., and so I will not deal with it directly in this volume.

assumption—that if there is such a plan, God wants us to know it and will reveal it to those who ask. They teach that God's sovereign plan for each life is intended to be the source and pattern of guidance for the individual.

The key distinctive in this traditional view is the role of the specific plan of God for the individual. Guidance, according to this view, occurs when God reveals that plan (or parts of it) through means such as inner impulses and promptings. F. B. Meyer summarizes this view in his concept of the "three lights." He says that there are three sources (lights) for guidance and they must all line up like navigation buoys in a great ocean.

> The circumstances of our daily life are to us an infallible indication of God's will, when they concur with the inward promptings of the Spirit and the Word of God. (Meyer 1896, 16)

This gradual unveiling of the divine plan is thought to be a normal and necessary part of the Christian life. Without it we might stray far away from the course God has intended for us (though we may stay within the boundaries of general biblical obedience). J. Oswald Sanders cites the case of the head of a large Bible college who, though he trained thousands of young people for the mission field, believed that he was experiencing God's second best. He was in a marriage that made it impossible for him to go to the foreign field (Sanders 1992, 27). Sanders attempts to criticize such a view because it leaves a Christian in an awkward spiritual position. The problem is that such a view flows by necessity from the traditional position. I am sure Sanders mentions it because it would be a problem for any person who held the traditional position yet had made mistakes in life-shaping choices.

Let me use a simple parable to illustrate this view of guidance (as well as the other two) and how it is granted by God. (Perhaps it is too simple, but I believe it will highlight the differences in the three views.) Let's say that you agree to house-sit for a wealthy couple who are going on safari in Africa. You offer to do some landscaping work while you are there. The owners are delighted and agree to the deal.

You arrive at the house on the appointed day and find, to your horror, that the couple has already gone. You discover a note thanking you in advance for the projects you will complete. The note, however, says nothing about which specific projects they want you to work on and you cannot contact them. Puzzled, you go the garage and notice that certain tools are already laid out for you. A particular type of fertilizer is opened. You also find some photos of some plantings at a local arboretum. From these and other clues you put together what you hope is a reconstruction of their plan for your work. But until they return, you cannot be totally sure that you implemented their plan and not your own. It all depends on whether or not you read the clues correctly.

In somewhat the same way, the traditional view of guidance requires us to interpret circumstances, our own inner senses and promptings, and the views of others to arrive at what we believe is God's plan for us. God does not directly show the plan to us. Therefore, great care must be taken to be accurate in our reading of it.

The Traditional Charismatic View

I will call the second view the "traditional charismatic view." This position is similar to the first one in that it also seeks guidance by obtaining knowledge of the individual and specific plan of God. The difference is that in this view, God communicates directly and verbally with individuals, families, and churches to let them know his plan for them. This often occurs through an apostle, prophet, prophecy, audible or inaudible voice, or a "word of knowledge." In this way believers can be sure that they are following God's plan and not their own.

In this case, the house sitter, instead of having to discern the clues, simply waits for a telephone call from Africa. When the call comes, he jots down the specifics and attacks his landscaping work with a much higher degree of confidence. He expects a direct verbal communication. He assumes that the couple in Africa would not let him guess about their plans, so he waits for the call before he begins any work.

The charismatic view of guidance involves the confidence that God normally and naturally communicates with us in clear human language. Prophecy and prophetic utterances are the clearest way he gives direct, inspired guidance. Sometimes gifted individuals give a "word of knowledge" revealing something that could not be known by ordinary human insight. Dreams and visions are also forms of direct communication from God to the Christian. In short, each means of revelation that God used to give us the Scriptures is still available to individual Christians today.

The Wisdom View

The third view is what I will call the wisdom view. This perspective holds that although God does have an individual and specific plan for every Christian, this plan is strictly secret. God does not normally reveal anything about it to us. He goes to great lengths to tell of its existence and its power to control life on earth, but we are never led to expect to know it. We might say it is information that, for now at least, is for God's use alone.

In this view, divine guidance has nothing to do with discerning this secret plan and using it to make decisions. Guidance is given by God when he gives us insight into issues and choices so that we make the decisions with divinely inspired wisdom. *Guidance comes, in short, by God making us wise.* In this view, there is no seeking for the clues or signs of God's plan; there is no need for a direct word spoken by prophecy, dream, or vision.

The wisdom view sees God as guiding his children *mediately,* not *immediately.* That is, his guidance is mediated by (comes through) the *illumination* of our minds and hearts by the Word of God. God's work of illumination is like turning on the lights in an unfamiliar room. Once the lights are on, you can see and walk confidently. Otherwise, you need someone to take you by the hand and lead you. In the illuminated room, you can guide yourself, yet you are totally dependent on the light. In the same way God's Spirit illumines our mind and heart, that we may see the world in that light and follow the right course.

In immediate guidance, by contrast, the guidance never comes *through* anything else (like our illuminated insight or thoughts); it is always God speaking directly to us. Immediate guidance requires no interpretation because it comes in the form of direct verbal communication. Interpreted prophecy, casting of lots, or an address by God in a dream would be immediate. Moses, for example, did not need to discern whether God wanted the children of Israel to break camp and move on; the glory cloud of Jehovah led them by moving. God could certainly guide immediately today if he wished. However, in the age of the Spirit, he chooses to guide mediately because of the illuminating power of that Spirit.

Put into the analogy of the house sitter, this view suggests that the homeowners might leave a video series on "Landscaping for the Homeowner." In addition, the couple would leave their journals and letters to let him know their tastes and personalities. But they would leave no specific directions for the landscape design. They would trust the house sitter to come up with his own plan based on the information they left. What the house sitter does not know is that the couple has done extensive research on him. They have chosen him because they know how he will react to the information they left behind. They left him only the commission to make the property a beautiful and fitting place for them. They want him to create his own design—which will nevertheless be just what they wanted. The homeowners have a distinct vision for their property, but it is fulfilled through the wisdom and gifts of their guest.

AS you can see, these views on how one seeks and receives guidance are very different, in theory and in practice. Little wonder that the very explosion of books on the subject of guidance, while meeting a need, also produces confusion. The story of my first experience with guidance could fit with any of these three views. What really did happen on that dirt path on my way home from school? If we are going to analyze each of these three positions biblically, we need to look first at four important topics: (1) the doctrine of providence, (2) the sufficiency of the Scripture, (3) the doctrine of illumination, and (4) the current work of the Holy Spirit. With that completed, we will be able to determine which of the three views is most consistent with Scripture, and we will return to our discussion of them.

For Review and Reflection

1. What are the three views of guidance described in this chapter? How would you summarize them?

2. Which view is most popular in your Christian circles?

3. Which view best describes your convictions? Why?

4. Have you been exposed to the "wisdom view" of guidance before reading this book? How do you react to it?

GUIDANCE AND THE
PROMISES OF GOD

IT had been three weeks since Alice's mother had moved in with Alice, her husband, and their two teenage children. Alice and her siblings all agreed that their mother could no longer maintain the home she had occupied for forty-five years. She needed assistance with many daily tasks but was fearful of entering an assisted living residence.

Alice, as a Christian, believed that children should do all they can to honor and care for their parents. Yet, since coming into the home, Alice's mother had done nothing but interfere with Alice's discipline and guidance of her teenage children. She voiced her disapproval of much that Alice said and did. When confronted about her behavior, Alice's mother agreed to change, but never did. The situation was difficult, but Alice struggled with guilt at the thought of putting her mother into an institution—even a good one. What should she do? She needed guidance from God.

Does the almighty God, the Maker of heaven and earth, actually promise to provide guidance to his small creatures? And if so, does that infinite, eternal God provide direction to *you*, one of about ten billion individuals who have lived on the planet Earth since creation?

The physical facts of the situation are not encouraging. Man seems very insignificant. The universe appears at present to be at least twelve billion light years across. Astronomers have gotten glimpses of what they think are galaxies 90 percent of the way across that expanse, and yet only 10 percent of that matter is visible across that distance. The universe is so vast that there is an entire galaxy (many containing millions of stars) for every grain of sand on the earth.

Then there are the unseen realms of heaven, created outside of time and space where untold myriads of angels and other created beings dwell. Against that backdrop, one person's decision about a mother's living situation, a job, a school, or a mate may seem incredibly insignificant outside the tiny, temporary sphere of our self-centered existence. Why would God be concerned with such fleeting details anyway? Why would it matter at all since everyone and everything ends up dead? Are we just living in denial, ignoring all the evidence for the insignificance of our decisions?

Biologist Stephen J. Gould is typical of modern thinkers who label our desires for significance as "beautiful illusion" (Gould 1996). Gould reminds us that scientifically speaking, bacteria could legitimately claim to be the highest form of life on the planet. After all, they are the ones who can survive in volcanos and inside rock, mutate to match any environment, and reproduce astronomically large numbers of offspring. If survival is the goal, bacteria reign supreme.

Sociobiologists propagate the idea that our genes are programmed to generate this illusion of significance to trick us into fighting for our existence; this in turn allows our genes to reproduce themselves. Others conclude that we are simply "over-evolved" and are therefore cursed with the illusion of significance. Perhaps that is what drives people's obsession with extraterrestrial life forms in space. Humanity without God has nothing higher or larger with which to link itself. Mankind is reduced to the sorry futility of listening for "god" on radio receivers with antennas the size of a football field, as if the discovery of more life would change the basic questions of our significance. But if alien life were found, our lives would then, from a secular perspective, be just that much more insignificant.

The Focus of God's Interest

So, does God care about those minute decisions we make on this speck of space dust we call Earth? Psalm 8:3–4 asks exactly that question.

> *When I consider your heavens,*
> *the work of your fingers,*
> *the moon and the stars,*
> *which you have set in place,*
> *what is man that you are mindful of him,*
> *the son of man that you care for him?*

The answer Psalm 8 gives is a powerful yes—God does care! Those who accept the God of the Bible as the author of life have a distinctive perception of the universe. We know from Scripture that God created time and space and all its contents. Creation had a definite beginning a certain number of years ago (opinions vary from six thousand to 17 billion years).

Even those scientists who initially believed in an eternal universe (Einstein, Hoyle, Jeans, and others) have reluctantly acknowledged that time, space, and matter began at a specific point in the past in an immense creative event (Ross 1991, 91).

But our significance is not just that we were created by God or that we are unique in the cosmos. It is, rather, that we are the image of God. Psalm 8:5 proclaims,

Chapter Three

You made him a little lower than the heavenly beings,
and crowned him with glory and honor.

As the Westminster Shorter Catechism reminds us, "The chief end of man is to glorify God and to enjoy him forever." The ability to relate to God is what defines us as human. The humble status of our physical size or power in such a universe only shows the majesty of God and the obvious point that we are totally dependent on him. The size of the universe and its display of God's power were never meant to gauge our significance, anyway. Rather, the glory we behold is created by God so that mankind might see *his* majesty and power.

The sheer size, mass, and unimaginable power currently observable in the cosmos is only overwhelming with respect to us. With respect to God himself, the cosmos is insignificant; it pales in comparison to the grandeur of its Author. The Christian instinctively understands this. He knows the cosmos would instantly disappear without the upholding and sustaining care of God. So whether Earth is the geographical "center" of the universe or whether it is somewhere else is irrelevant. It is God and the meaning he gives to his creation that alone define human existence and the meaning of individual lives.

Scripture teaches that God's purpose for humankind began even before creation (Eph. 1:4–6). It spans the aeons and centers in the reformation of the cosmos and humanity through a man, Jesus Christ (Eph. 1:9–10). The question we must return to is this: Does this overall purpose of God mean that he guides individuals like you or me in specific decisions?

We would be comforted and strengthened to think so. Yet that does not automatically make it a reality. Most pagan cultures have established methods to divine the "will of the gods." Dr. Bruce Waltke, in his fine book, *Finding the Will of God,* has done a powerful job of comparing pagan divination rites to methods Christians are tempted to use to find the will of God. Rulers of all ages have sought and claimed divine direction for their policies and wars. Common ordinary folks are tempted to look for signs of approval and backing for decisions we have already made (or want to make). Nebuchadnezzar of Babylon (Dan. 1–4), for example, supported a stable of wise men, astrologers, and seers to guide him in his decisions, and the Greeks had their Oracle at Delphi. The Africans had witch doctors to discern the will of departed ancestral spirits and American Indians had their shamans. The human race naturally turns to higher spiritual powers—either to submit to them, as to the true God, or to use them, as is usual in pagan religion.

Many devout Christians have, in fact, maintained that God does not really guide us (at least in the normal sense of that word). Rather, they would say, he has clearly revealed his will and purpose—love God and love one another. It is up to us to "link" our lives to those purposes (Sine 1987, 131–56). In that sense, all the guidance content we need has been given in the Bible. In their view, an eight-year-old boy who understands "Love your neighbor as yourself" has all the guidance he needs for life. Thus there is no need for individualized guidance—only personal decision making. While there is a profound truth in this, we shall see that it does not do justice to the personal care and leading we find promised in Scripture. God, I believe, does far more than reveal his general purposes and then leave us to link ourselves to them or pragmatically calculate the most edifying outcomes.

Most of us who have spent time in biblically committed churches have become accustomed to the idea that God is concerned for our individual guidance. Is this a hangover from pagan religion? Is it just the cry of a heart that does not want to submit to the revealed purposes of God? Or is it just a reflection of our overly individualistic culture? We shall see that it is none of these.

As Christians we recognize that we should not project onto God the qualities we desire. Rather, we ought to examine carefully what he has revealed about himself and then base our lives on that. We look to the Bible as the "only infallible rule of faith and practice," the full self-disclosure of God in human language. To be consistent, therefore, a Christian must ask, "Does God really give specific guidance to those who follow him?" Does he promise to lead and guide Christians today? We receive direction and advice from parents, pastors, Christian friends, and mentors, but does God himself promise to provide this?

I believe that the Bible gives a clear answer to this question. That answer is *yes*. Without concerning ourselves (for a few pages) with *how* God guides, let's look at some of the passages that teach that God leads us.

Guidance of the Patriarchs

In Genesis 12:1, God commands Abraham to leave Ur and go to a "land I will show you." He actually directs Abraham across the Fertile Crescent some eight hundred miles to Canaan. The story of Abraham, Isaac, Jacob, and Joseph is one in which God allows us to see him as Guide and Leader. He lets us see how he arranged circumstances when Joseph was sold as a slave in Egypt (Gen. 50:20). He also showed himself as one who leads by clear verbal direction, as when he commanded Abraham to sacrifice Isaac (Gen. 22:1). In Genesis 26:2 God appeared to Abraham and told him to leave immediately for Egypt because of an upcoming famine. God guided Abraham's servant to an individual woman (Rebekah) in Chaldea, hundreds of miles away, in order to obtain a wife for Isaac (Gen. 24). God spoke to Jacob at Bethel, renewing his covenant promises, even as Jacob fled from Esau (Gen. 27:41). God appeared to Jacob at Peniel and blessed him after an all-night wrestling match. God's guidance was a decisive factor in the lives of all the patriarchs.

By the time of Jacob, God began to be called "The Shepherd, the Rock of Israel" (Gen. 49:24). The concept of shepherd combined the power of protection, the security of provision, and the comfort of guidance and direction. When Jacob blessed Joseph, he referred to the God of Abraham as "the God who has been my Shepherd all my life to this day." The patriarchs visibly and consciously enjoyed the blessings of their Shepherd through the unique covenant relationship God had with them.

Guidance Under the Law

Through the Exodus, God's revelation of himself as Guide and Leader took on colossal proportions as he liberated Israel out of Egypt. Exodus 13:21–22 records,

> *By day the LORD went ahead of them in a pillar of cloud to guide them on their way and by night in a pillar of fire to give them light, so that they could travel by day or night. Neither the pillar of cloud by day nor the pillar of fire by night left its place in front of the people.*

Just picture two million people walking through the desert following this majestic, protective, life-giving cloud, heading for a direct verbal encounter with God himself in the Sinai Peninsula! When the cloud moved, Israel moved. When it stopped, they stopped (Num. 9:15–17). What a powerful picture of God himself guiding his people. Now, that is dramatic, immediate guidance!

When the people arrived at Mount Sinai, God established Moses as the mediator of his relationship with Israel. God spoke to him as a "man speaks to his friend" (Ex. 33:11; Num. 12:6–8). God appointed Moses so that the people would be spared the trauma of directly hearing his own voice. God made a covenant with them, giving extensive guidance about every aspect of their life and salvation. This is all recorded in the Torah, the five books of the law.

In addition, God provided through the priesthood the Urim and the Thummim. With these, the priest could ask a question of God and receive a yes or no answer. They were objects carried over the heart in the breastplate of the priest (Ex. 28:30; Lev. 8:8). Scholars do not know exactly what they were or how they rendered yes or no answers, yet they were a gift of God by which the priest could inquire of the Lord for direction in doubtful cases (Davis 1924, 795). The Lord instructed Moses to commission Joshua to have access to the Urim so that he also could receive direction from Jehovah during the conquest of Canaan. This powerful tool could be used anywhere the high priest was present—on the battlefield, in the courtroom, or in the temple. Again, God makes dramatic provisions to express his character as their Guide.

The shepherd theme continues in Numbers 27:15–17, as the aging Moses records a beautiful prayer asking God for a leader to take his place "so the LORD's people will not be like a sheep without a shepherd" (v. 17). This is the first reference to God's people as a flock of sheep needing to be led by a shepherd. It harks back to the gracious blessings of God to Abraham, Isaac, and Jacob as their Shepherd. Moses wanted the same blessings for the people as a whole. It introduces one of the primary pictures of God's relationship to his growing body.

Guidance in the Psalms and Prophets

Sinclair Ferguson captures this theme well in the opening chapter of his fine book *Discovering the Will of God* (Ferguson 1982, 9). He says,

> From earliest years, perhaps, you have been able to say: "The Lord is my Shepherd . . . He leads me . . ." (Ps. 23:1–2). Certainly during your Christian life, if you are a Christian, there have been many situations in which you have turned to the

Lord and said: "I do not know what to do here, help me!" You have proved his guiding hand in the large and small affairs of life. Yes, you need guidance. Yes, God has promised to be your Guide. Yes, God has undoubtedly guided you already.

Psalm 23 is one of the clearest texts in which God promises personal guidance. The Maker of heaven and earth gives himself to us as Shepherd. The blessing of God to Abraham, Isaac, and Jacob is claimed by the Psalmist. God allows you and me to call him *my* shepherd; to confess that he leads *me* beside still waters; he guides *me* in paths of righteousness. God is not just our Guide; he is *my* Guide. There is no ultimate tension between God as our God and God as my God.

The Psalms abound in references to our personal relationship to God as Guide and Leader.

Lead me, O LORD, in your righteousness
 because of my enemies—
make straight your way before me. (5:8)

Teach me your way, O LORD;
 lead me in a straight path
 because of my oppressors. (27:11)

Since you are my rock and my fortress,
 for the sake of your name lead and guide me. (31:3)

For this God is our God for ever and ever;
 he will be our guide even to the end. (48:14)

If I rise on the wings of the dawn,
 if I settle on the far side of the sea,
even there your hand will guide me. (139:9–10)

It is interesting to note that the psalms reflecting the keenest and most personal guidance are psalms of David, the forerunner of Christ. Other psalmists reflect this confidence (Korah in Ps. 48:14), but David's messianic role most clearly reminds us of Christ's own relationship to God, a relationship Christ offers us through his death and resurrection. In chapters 4–5 we will explore the significance this has for those who are united to Christ. We will look at the way God has opened to us Christ's own access to the Father.

In the prophets we return to the language of the Shepherd. Isaiah 40:11 says,

> He [the coming messiah] tends his flock like a shepherd: He
> 		gathers the lambs in his arms
> and carries them close to his heart;
> he gently leads those that have young.
>
> They will . . . find pasture on every barren hill . . .
> He who has compassion on them will guide them
> and lead them beside springs of water. (Isa. 49:9–10)

Isaiah 58:11 reminds Israel that if they show compassion and break the yoke of oppression, then "the LORD will guide you always; he will satisfy you in a sun-scorched land."

Guidance in the Gospels

Certainly the Old Testament saints hoped for the coming of the Shepherd, the divine Son of David, who once again would directly shepherd his sheep (Mic. 5:2). The Magi from the East quote Micah 5:2 in Matthew 2:6 saying,

> But you, Bethlehem, in the land of Judah,
> 		are by no means least among the rulers of Judah;

for out of you will come a ruler
  who will be the shepherd of my people Israel.

The Lord will shepherd not in the fearful thundering from Mount Sinai, but in grace and mercy. Christ comes upon the scene confidently revealing himself to be that Shepherd. The God of Abraham, the Shepherd of Israel, has come to lay down his life for the sheep.

The apostle John beautifully relays this message of Jesus in John 10:1–18. The Shepherd knows each of the sheep by name, calls them by name, and leads them out to pasture. As they travel toward the pasture, he walks ahead of them, guiding and protecting. Then in verse 11, and again in verse 14, he identifies himself as the true Shepherd. He reveals that he has other sheep "not of this fold" (v. 16) but that he is also their Shepherd, so that there is "one flock and one shepherd." Hebrews 13:20 calls Jesus "that great Shepherd of the sheep." Peter calls elders to accountability because the "Chief Shepherd" will appear (1 Peter 5:4).

This metaphor is a powerful picture of Christ's guidance and leadership. Christ makes us part of his flock, but he knows and calls each of us by name. We are given the picture of a flock dispersed on a hillside with the shepherd walking among the sheep, calling each by name to divert them away from danger and toward good pasture. Maybe that is a good picture of the church during the week, dispersed in the world, yet cared for by Christ in a very personal way. The gathered church more closely resembles the picture of the shepherd leading a compact column of sheep on a road toward pasture or the safety of the sheep pen. There is a marvelous balance here between visualizing each sheep as precious to Christ and yet having a common identity in his one flock. God's guidance is individual, but not individualistic. His guidance takes full account of the relationship we sustain with the whole body of Christ, the church.

Guidance After Pentecost

After Christ accomplished redemption by his death and resurrection, he returned to his Father in Heaven and sent the Holy Spirit. The Spirit's work was to take the benefits won by Christ and to give them practically to individual men and women who trust him as Savior. This Spirit would complete the work for the reigning Shepherd. Everything Christ does after Pentecost and prior to the Second Coming he does through his Spirit (John 16:14–15). The Holy Spirit thus transmits the blessings of God's guidance to us.

Jesus was the first to receive the Holy Spirit when John baptized him at the Jordan river. Luke 4:1 says, "Jesus, full of the Holy Spirit, returned from the Jordan and was led by the Spirit in the desert." The word "led" is a very strong word, much closer to our words *driven* or *taken*. It is most commonly used to describe a prisoner being "led" to court or to punishment (Luke 22:24, 26 and dozens of similar references). That sense fits the description of Christ being led into the wilderness, not as Israel was led to meet God, but to meet Satan and suffer horrible temptations. Yet clearly the Holy Spirit is the means for guiding and leading Christ.

Paul uses a similar expression to describe guidance in Romans 8:14: "Those who are led by the Spirit of God are the sons of God." This startling passage promises the leading of the Spirit to every single child of God. It is the mark of sonship; the Spirit of sonship cries "Abba Father" (Rom. 8:15). It is that Spirit who testifies to our spirit that we are the sons of God. Knowing that we are God's is, of course, the most important "guidance" a Christian can ever experience.

In Romans 12:2 Paul says, "Do not conform any longer to the pattern of this world, but be transformed by the renewing of your mind. Then you will be able to test and approve what God's will is—his good, pleasing and perfect will." Knowing God's will is the fruit of a transformed mind. We will give specific attention to this passage in chapter 5. Suffice it to say, God does hold out to us the prospect of testing and approving the will of God. Such knowledge is not so much a fortune cookie as it is an education.

In Colossians 1:9–12, Paul prays that the Christian would be filled with the knowledge of God's will in order that they would "please him in every way: bearing fruit in every good work" (1:10). No one could ask for more guidance than that, or for a more completely satisfactory outcome to his life. Similar language is used by Paul in Philippians 1:9–10: "And this is my prayer: that your love may abound more and more in knowledge and depth of insight, so that you may be able to discern what is best and may be pure and blameless until the day of Christ." Paul strongly believed that this kind of discernment was available to Christians from God through prayer.

James 1:5 promises that "if any of you lacks wisdom, he should ask God, who gives generously to all." We will look at this passage in more detail later, but for now realize that God is offering to all believers the blessing of wisdom. It is a wisdom from God; it is from above (James 3:17), and it enables the Christian to reap a harvest of righteousness. The condition for bestowing this wisdom is that Christians "believe and not doubt."

This survey of passages demonstrates that God does indeed guide us, both as individuals and as his corporate body. He continues to be the "Great Shepherd of the Sheep," our Leader and Guide. Despite the great gulf between heaven and earth, despite our small spot in the universe, despite our natural disregard for God, those in Christ are guided. It is because of the work of Jesus Christ that God guides us. He guides not just in the crises of life or the exceptional experiences, but in "every good work." We can say with King David, "The LORD is my shepherd. . . . Surely goodness and mercy will follow me all the days of my life" (Ps. 23:1, 6).

DO you have a guided life? Have you experienced the shepherding of Christ? Do you know the "quiet waters" of God's guidance in the midst of the upheavals of our culture? The rod and staff of God can be yours as you face the intensely competitive, downsized, make-or-break world we have created for ourselves. Paul said it well in 2 Corinthians 4:8:

> *We are hard pressed on every side, but not crushed; perplexed, but not in despair; persecuted, but not abandoned; struck down, but not destroyed.*

The apostle Paul went through enormous stress as he sought to fulfill his calling from God. But his relationship to God is in essence no different from that of Christians today. Paul had a purpose to glorify God and a calling to serve him. His plans expressed his assignment from God. Against it were many obstacles, imprisonments, sicknesses, betrayals, and dead ends. Yet Paul completed his life assignments confident that he had done the will of God. He says in 2 Timothy 4:7, "I have fought the good fight, I have finished the race, I have kept the faith."

Do you want to be able to say that too? If you are one who seeks to glorify and serve God, that can be the outcome of your life as well. If you have submitted your heart to God's purposes for your life, you can share Paul's confidence that God will guide you through all the seasons of your life. We will look at how God does this in the next chapter.

For Review and Reflection

1. What situations make you feel meaningless and insignificant in the grand scheme of things? What does the Bible say to combat that mentality?

2. Independently review the Scripture passages mentioned in this chapter. Do you think that the conclusion is valid: namely, that God does guide his people—collectively and individually?

3. What objections to that conclusion do you see? Write them down and see if they are answered in the rest of the book.

PART TWO   *Understanding Guidance*

CHAPTER

GUIDANCE AND THE
PLAN OF GOD

RICK was a talented graphic designer I met some years ago. He had about ten years of experience working for a successful advertising agency, but he chafed at the atmosphere of cutthroat competition among employees scrambling to "make partner." He also recoiled at the low moral tone and the heavy pressure to produce. He naturally wondered if he could do just as well on his own, yet he was fearful of trying to compete with his old firm for business. He dreamed that if he could begin his own firm, he would finally have control over his life. He could set his own hours and be more involved in ministry. Yet he also had a wife with three small children. If he failed at his attempt to go solo, everyone would suffer. He might lose his house and savings.

Rick prayed that he might be shown the plan of God for his life. He asked God whether that plan called for him to start his own firm or stay put. He began to look for ways God might be trying to communicate with him. He looked for potential customers who might appear in rather unusual ways. He began to listen for God's voice in his own thoughts—some special divine "tag" that might make a thought stand out as from God. He wondered if there were some tests that he could employ to decide the issue. For example, if there was unusual slander, gossip, and other forms of evil at work on the anniversary of his conversion to Christ, perhaps that would be a sign that the place was just too corrupt.

As he meditated on this, a disturbing thought began to intrude into his mind. He was not sure, but he feared he had missed God's plan for his life back in college. He had gone to the Urbana Student Missionary Convention and signed up to pursue missions, but once he got back to school, he was easily talked out of it by his faculty advisor. What would have happened if he had used his communication abilities to spread the gospel instead of creating advertisements? Perhaps he was now so far from God's will for his life that it was pointless to try to get back to it, much less ask God to guide him within his current, "disobedient" plan.

Rick's problems in seeking guidance from God are very common among Christians. For Rick and for many others, their understanding of the plan and will of God has never been sharpened by biblical concepts. One of Rick's major problems is confusing two very different uses of the term "the will of God" in the Bible.

In Scripture, the phrase "the will of God" can mean either the *plan* of God or the *commandments* of God. Theologians describe them as the two wills of God: his "decretive will" (his decrees or plan) and his "preceptive will" (his precepts or commands) (Hodge 1865, 1:405). The *decretive* will of God directs everything that happens under God's control over the world. The *preceptive* will has to do with God's precepts—what he calls or commands *us* to do. Since the Bible uses the phrase "will of God" in both these senses, it is easy to confuse them. That in turn leads to confusion in our search for guidance. That was one of Rick's problems.

To help you avoid this pitfall, let's examine both biblical concepts of the will of God. In this chapter we will look at the "will of God" as it refers to God's sovereign plan (his decrees or his decretive will, as it is sometimes called in theology). In the next chapter we will examine the "will of God" as God's commandments.

The Will of God: His Plan

Scripture often uses the phrase "will of God" to refer to God's plan. God's sovereign plan is referred to in Ephesians 1:5 where Paul says, "He [God] predestined us . . . in accordance with his pleasure and *will.*" Every believer in Christ should have the comfort of knowing that he or she was chosen before creation to inherit salvation. That choice was made by God in his sovereign plan. Paul continues the theme in Ephesians 1:11 where he declares, "In him we were also chosen, having been predestined according to the plan of him who works out everything in conformity *with the purpose of his will.*"

James 4:15 is another example of this usage. James exhorts his readers not to make their own plans with a spirit of self-assurance (to go to a city, live and make money there) but rather to say, *"If it is the Lord's will,* we will live and do this or that." James does not condemn planning; he condemns planning that does not leave room for God's plan. James tells us not to set our heart on our plans because our life is like a vapor, here today and gone tomorrow.

In Romans 15:32, Paul applies James's teaching. He asks the Romans to pray "so that *by God's will* I may come to you with joy and together with you be refreshed." Paul wants to come to the Roman Christians but recognizes that he can only come by the providence and plan of God; that is, if God has already ordained it.

If we were to impose the other sense of the term "will of God" on this passage, it would make no sense. Paul is not asking the Romans to pray so that *he* would do the will of God (i.e., fulfill God's commands). Rather Paul wants them to pray that God would permit him to come to Rome by providing the circumstances to make it possible.

One last example: Peter uses the phrase "will of God" in this sense in 1 Peter 3:17. "It is better, *if it is God's will,* to suffer for doing good than for doing evil." While urging Christians to suffer for doing good rather than suffer for doing evil, he makes the side point that suffering itself comes through the plan and permission of God. Therefore, he refers to suffering that may come "if it is God's will." Again, we are confronted with the outworking of God's plan.

Rick not only confused the two terms, but his confusion entangled him in what I call the "Plan B Syndrome." Rick's logic went like this: If God has a fixed, detailed plan for the life of each believer and he wants us to follow that plan, what do we do when we stray from it? Well, we drop down to Plan B and have to take it from there.

Let me illustrate. Every year I go through the same agonizing routine of deciding which plan I will choose for the service contract on my very old oil burner. Plan A, according to our friendly fuel oil dealer, will rid me from all cares. Under that plan they will fix everything but, of course, it costs more. Plan B is more reasonably priced, but only covers common problems. Plan C gives me an annual cleanout but no repairs whatsoever. If I have some money in the bank, I tend to choose Plan A. If I am short on money (broke), I choose C, and that, of course, is the year that the repairman might just as well camp out at my house.

In the same way, we tend to think that while God has a "best" plan for our life, he also has some other, "cheaper" plans for people who miss the best. We remember certain foolish or sinful decisions we've made and, because of the consequences, see ourselves on a permanent "Plan B" regarding God's will for our lives. Each time we make another bad decision, we drop down a notch to Plan C, Plan D, and—being the sinners that we are—we soon run out of letters in the alphabet. We think of "what could have been" if we hadn't married so-and-so, had not gotten pregnant before marriage, had not taken this horrible job and turned down the one that would have made our career, or had not blown up at our teenage son.

In this chapter we will see that for those who are in Christ, there is only one plan, Plan A. This plan holds despite all our stupid mistakes and sins. We shall see the wonder of God's shepherding care, the detail of his love through his decreed plan for our lives. It is at once a truth that is awe-inspiring, deeply comforting, and yet sometimes intimidating for us, God's proud creatures.

One Sovereign Plan

The Bible teaches that (1) God does have one specific plan for your life and (2) the events and choices of your life irresistibly and sovereignly work that plan in every detail. Contrary to Rick's view of God's plan, one cannot "flunk out" of it. It has all your mistakes, blindnesses, and sins accounted for in advance. These truths are included in what is known as the doctrine of God's providence. Without understanding providence, we will never be able to think clearly about God's daily involvement with our lives. Much of the confusion about God's guidance in Christian circles is caused by a lack of understanding of this historic doctrine.

The doctrine of providence was brilliantly summarized in 1648 in the Westminster Confession of Faith (a document foundational to the theology of English-speaking Congregational, Reformed, Presbyterian, and many Baptist churches). Chapter 5 is entitled "Of Providence" and begins as follows:

> God the great Creator of all things doth uphold, direct, dispose, and govern all creatures, actions, and things, from the greatest even to the least, by His most wise and holy providence, according to His infallible fore-knowledge, and the free and im-

> mutable counsel of His own will, to the praise of the glory of
> His wisdom, power, justice, goodness, and mercy.

This statement summarizes the answer to many questions that arise as we try to understand what the Bible says about God's control of our world. Notice particularly that this doctrine affirms that God works every detail "according to the immutable [unchangeable] counsel of his own will." If that is true, it has far-reaching implications for Rick as he evaluates his alternatives. He does not have to climb out of the hole he dug for himself to get back into God's will for his life. His history, and the decisions that created it, were *within* God's redemptive plan for him.

If this is true, it validates the decision making he must now do, because he is not stuck in some second- or twentieth-best situation. He stands on the platform of the perfect and wise decrees of God's providence. He is not like a golfer who must step up to the first tee with a twenty-stroke penalty. If this doctrine is true, it provides significant hope as we make decisions about our lives.

But before we look further at the implications of this truth, we must ask, "Is this really true?" And if it is true, what about human responsibility and freedom? What about the problems caused by our sin and stupidity? What about the problem of evil in the world? Does that make God the originator of evil? Let's examine some key biblical passages upon which the doctrine of providence is based. They will help us understand providence's implications for many important areas of our lives.

Circumstances

Does God control all circumstances in all situations? Christ himself answers that question in Matthew 10:29–31. Jesus says that "not one of them [sparrows] will fall to the ground apart from the will of your

Father. And even the very hairs of your head are all numbered." Jesus goes on to use this extraordinary level of care and control by God to allay his disciples' fears when facing persecution and testing. Things that seem accidental (finding a dead bird by your sidewalk) do not take place without the permission of God. He says, "So don't be afraid; you are worth more than many sparrows" (v. 31).

Notice the purpose of Jesus' teaching. He did not give it to establish an abstract principle that could be applied in any direction we might fancy. He gave it to minister to the fear of loss, death, suffering, abuse, etc., among his people. It clearly establishes the total and sovereign control of God over life, but the doctrine has a pastoral purpose, which must be respected.

Some might ask, "How can I receive comfort from a doctrine that teaches that everything is determined and implies that there is no use to prayer or human effort?" Non-Christians might object and say, "Why should I accept a view that makes God the cause of evil?" Their mistake is to look at the doctrine as an isolated truth that can turn any way the logic of their minds leads them. The doctrine of God's sovereign control over circumstances is never used in Scripture to discourage prayer or human effort but rather the exact reverse. *Because* God can intervene, we should pray and we should work. It is never used to establish God's authorship of evil. In fact, that is explicitly denied in James 1:13 and many other passages. Satan and mankind's own sin are identified as the causes of all evil.

Let's look at the purposes for which this doctrine is actually used in Scripture. Its purposes are to induce humility in God's creatures (Rom. 9:20), to generate praise for God's unconstrained love for sinners (Eph. 1:11), to assure believers of the indestructibility and practicality of God's love (Rom. 8:28), and to warn enemies of the futility of resistance and rebellion (Ps. 2:9–10; Dan. 4:34–35). This doctrine highlights the facts that our individuality and seasons of life are ordained by God (Ps. 139:13–16). David reflects on the great personal value of knowing that God constantly had thoughts of him. He says,

> *How vast is the sum of them!*
> *Were I to count them,*
> *they would outnumber the grains of sand.*
> *(Ps. 139:17–18)*

How many of us really believe that the God we worship is that aware of the circumstances of our lives? That he is thinking of our circumstances in more detail than we ever could? David says that we could not even count God's thoughts, much less pay such abundant, detailed attention to our own circumstances. I weep for Christians who have concluded that they cannot enjoy this confidence in God's providence for fear of implicating him in evil.

We may have had experiences with some who misuse the doctrine of providence. They are like the strongly Calvinistic man (one who believes God controls all things) who fell down a long flight of stairs one morning on his way to breakfast. "Fortunately" the stairs were carpeted, and he was able to get up, dust himself off, and slowly hobble to the breakfast table. He sat down, looked at his wife, and said, "Boy, am I glad that's over." While in a logical (and humorous) sense that response might be appealing, it only diverts attention from this man's duty to figure out what went wrong and take precautions against future falls. God did not reveal the reality of his providential care to turn us away from being stewards of our lives. Close calls like that sometimes do, however, remind us of God's unseen care.

I once heard a story about John Witherspoon, the president of Princeton University and signer of the Declaration of Independence. One day Witherspoon was thrown from his carriage on the way to work at Princeton. The carriage landed in a ditch, and he was sprawled out on the ground, covered with dirt. When he arrived at the office, he began cleaning himself up and commented on the marvelous providence of God that protected his life in a very dangerous situation. His young assistant wisely observed, "But Dr. Witherspoon, was not God's care even more marvelous on the hundreds of mornings when you have not even come close to an accident?" Witherspoon learned a valuable lesson about thanksgiving for God's providence when it is less visible and dramatic.

A beautiful illustration of God's providence is recorded in Genesis 50:20. Up to that point, Genesis tells the story of how Joseph's brothers sold him into slavery, how Joseph was falsely accused of rape and unjustly imprisoned, how he rose to great power in Egypt and then saved Egypt and his family from starvation. After all this, in Genesis 50:20 Joseph tells his brothers why he will not take revenge on them for their treachery. He says, "You intended to harm me, but God intended it for good to accomplish what is now being done, the saving of many lives." Every action of the brothers, of Joseph, of Pharaoh, and even of the weather that brought the famine, was according to the sovereign control of God.

There is, in short, no circumstance—from the numbering of the hairs of our heads to the great movements of nations—that does not in every respect work out the plan of God.

If we grant that circumstances are determined by the providence of God, what about the results of directly evil acts by mankind? The story of Joseph previews the answer.

Good Men, Evil Men, and Politicians

Is God's plan worked out by the free and responsible actions of men and women, whether good or evil? It is the question evoked by Hitler, Pol Pot, and the thug who assaulted your child. It is the question of

63

Bishop Wilberforce and Martin Luther King, who fought for the rights and dignity of those of African descent.

This is a natural question in view of the reality of the Last Judgment, which clearly holds every man, woman, and child accountable for their own actions. John 5:28–29 says,

> *Do not be amazed at this, for a time is coming when all who are in their graves will hear his voice and come out—those who have done good will rise to live, and those who have done evil will rise to be condemned.*

What is implied by the story of Joseph is specifically taught in Scripture: that every act of every individual is according to the unchangeable blueprint of God. The Bible emphasizes the fact that the most "free" of all people (kings and rulers) work the plan of God. Proverbs 21:1 declares, "The king's heart is in the hand of the Lord; He directs it like a watercourse wherever he pleases." Other Scriptures carry the same message of God's sovereignty:

> *The plans of the Lord stand forever,*
> *the purposes of his heart through all generations.*
> *(Ps. 33:11)*

> *For the Lord Almighty has purposed, and who can thwart*
> *him?*
> *His hand is stretched out, and who can turn it back?*
> *(Isa. 14:27)*

> *Remember the former things, those of long ago;*
> *I am God, and there is no other;*
> *I am God, and there is none like me.*

I make known the end from the beginning,
* from ancient times, what is still to come.*
I say: My purpose will stand,
* and I will do all that I please. (Isa. 46:9–10)*

Many are the plans in a man's heart,
* but it is the LORD's purpose that prevails. (Prov. 19:21)*

No act of God's enemies or powerful rulers has any effect on his ability to carry out every last detail of his plan. In fact, their acts are no more insulated from God's ordained plan than were the futile acts of the great Pharaoh of Exodus who opposed Moses. Romans 9:17 records God speaking to Pharaoh and saying, "I raised you up for this very purpose, that I might display my power in you and that my name might be proclaimed in all the earth." It is interesting to note that the Exodus account of Pharaoh's rebellion says both that God hardened Pharaoh's heart (Ex. 14:4) and that Pharaoh hardened his own heart (Ex. 9:34). Pharaoh acted of his own responsible will, and yet his will worked the eternal purposes of God.

God's sovereignty over the evil acts of people comes to purest expression in Peter's sermon in Acts 2:23. "This man [Jesus] was handed over to you by God's set purpose and foreknowledge; and you, with the help of wicked men, put him to death by nailing him to the cross." Notice how Peter proclaims that even this arch crime of human history was ordained by the set purpose of God. Yet Peter is bold in laying responsibility for the crime directly on the religious leaders of Israel.

That human acts are covered by God's plan is comforting in a daily way to me. My wife is currently a campus staff worker with InterVarsity Christian Fellowship. She is out late on campus three or four nights a week (our children are grown). Recently, a student was abducted from a sidewalk at about eight o'clock one night. My wife had walked on that very spot ten minutes before. The student was taken to a vacant parking lot and raped. Under such circumstances, I am concerned about my wife being out late so many nights a week and we have taken a number of precautions. But our comfort is ultimately in the knowledge that no one, not even a hardened rapist, can touch her without God's redemptive plan being in force at that moment.

You might ask, "Isn't that impossible, that God could be in control, yet humans are the causes of good and evil?" It is evidently not impossible for God. Our minds cannot fathom how God can create responsible creatures who are truly accountable to him, while all their sin, from Adam in the Garden to the final death pangs of Satan, are worked out in strict accordance with the plan of God. Life is under control, but of a most sophisticated sort, beyond the range of human comprehension. With our own responsible wills, we work the plan of God, even though God does not tempt or directly coerce our wills in any way. Although we do not know how God controls all things, it appears that he generally keeps "hands off" the mechanism of our wills. Yet we responsibly and with freedom choose to do everything as he planned it.

I have heard so many believers say to me over the years, "You can't have it both ways; either humans are fully accountable for their actions or God's plan is in control." We must energetically resist the suggestion that since we can't understand how he does it, we must choose either responsibility or divine sovereignty; one or the other, but not both.

The fact that both are true is the very glory of God's wisdom. We should bow and worship, not be carried away with our arrogant musings about what God can and cannot do. We are finite creatures and do not have access to the level of thought or existence enjoyed by God. It is actually the epitome of logic and good sense to trust his revelation of himself. We should enjoy the fullness of God's glorious providence and the comfort of his mysterious, sovereign control. It should lead us to respond with awe as those who know they are accountable, as image-bearers of God.

Not only do evil acts fall within the providence of God, but the good acts of men are also foreordained. Ephesians 2:10 says, "We are God's workmanship, created in Christ Jesus to do good works, which God prepared in advance for us to do." Yet again and again we are *commanded* to do good works (1 Tim. 6:18; Heb. 10:24). In Philippians 2:12–13, Paul pulls back the curtain of metaphysics and lets us see the two realities functioning together. He says, "Work out your salvation with fear and trembling, for it is God who works in you to will and to act according to his good purpose." Rather than reducing human responsibility for the Christian, this truth amplifies it by linking it to an irresistible power—God working his good purpose in us. From here we look at God's providence at work in our salvation.

God's Providence in Salvation and Judgment

In this area of providence we step onto the holiest of ground. We are immediately humbled by the wonder and terror of what we read. If we approach the classic Scripture passages regarding "predestination" and take them at face value, it is amazingly clear that believers are such because they were chosen by God. We chose him because he chose us. Here are some of the verses that teach this:

In love he predestined us to be adopted as his sons through Jesus Christ. (Eph. 1:5)

You did not choose me, but I chose you . . . to go and bear fruit— fruit that will last. (John 15:16)

All that the Father gives me will come to me, and whoever comes to me I will never drive away. . . . And this is the will of him who

67

sent me, that I shall lose none of all that he has given me, but raise them up at the last day. (John 6:37, 39)

In these verses Jesus reveals that God gave him a distinct group of those to save, and every single one of them would actually be saved. Notice how Jesus balances his teaching by saying that everyone who comes to him desiring salvation will find it. He will turn no one away. It is both exclusive and personal, yet at the same time open to all. Here again is that glorious paradox created by the multi-leveled and (to us) mysterious way God governs his creatures. He has an eternal, unchangeable plan, which nothing can frustrate, yet God can create a world with true responsibility and dignity.

The way in which God plans salvation for his chosen ones and then completes it for every last one of them is captured in Romans 8:28–30.

And we know that in all things God works for the good of those who love him, who have been called according to his purpose. For those God foreknew, he also predestined to be conformed to the likeness of his Son, that he might be the firstborn among many brothers. And those he predestined, he also called; those he called, he also justified; those he justified, he also glorified.

The entire time line of our salvation—from before creation until final glorification—is according to "God's purpose." Everyone who is foreknown (looked upon in compassion, cf. Rom. 11:2) is predestined, and everyone predestined ends up glorified. No one falls out of the system.

Romans goes a step further and states that even those who never repent and are judged for their hatred of God do so according to the plan of God, set down prior to creation.

Romans 9:11, speaking of Rebekah's children (Jacob and Esau), says, "Yet, before the twins were born or had done anything good or bad—in order that God's purpose in election might stand: . . . she was told, 'The older will serve the younger.' . . . Jacob I loved, but Esau I hated." Paul goes on to give the purpose for revealing this truth in verse 16: "It does not, therefore, depend on man's desire or effort, but on God's mercy."

Paul is not revealing some philosophical capstone which creative minds can use in any way they want. No, he is pulling back the curtain on God's throne room that we might see the utter extent to which our salvation is by grace alone, originating in the pure and personal love of God for us. Again, all we can do is worship.

While we may find it difficult to assimilate this strong medicine for human pride, it need not be overwhelming when we use the doctrine *within the pastoral purpose for which it was revealed.* I must say again that theological truths, no matter how biblical, must be used in a biblical way. They are not bullets one can shoot in any direction, but only the directions revealed in Scripture.

We cannot, for instance, use God's right to choose as a reason to deny human responsibility or to convince ourselves that our efforts at witnessing to or praying for unbelievers are meaningless. On the contrary, it is God's very control and predestination that gives us hope that he will act. It is our reason to pray that God will save them. God can save or justly condemn and he has the authority and power to do either.

Paul mirrors the right attitude toward his unsaved Jewish kinsmen.

I speak the truth in Christ—I am not lying, my conscience confirms it in the Holy Spirit—I have great sorrow and unceasing anguish in my heart. For I could wish that I myself were cursed and cut off from Christ for the sake of my brothers, those of my own race, the people of Israel. (Rom. 9:1–2)

Paul understands our struggle and voices the anguish we feel as we consider the lost condition of people we love. But he responds to this desire for their salvation by fearlessly preaching to his Jewish brethren in every city and praying for them to be saved (Rom. 10:1).

The plan and purpose of God worked out in providence is a huge, unseen reality—active every minute protecting, guiding, and determining the flow of our destiny. If you are in Christ, you have the right to trust yourself to the eternal, unchangeable will of God, which undergirds your daily life. You are in an invisible harmony with God's plan for your life. There is no Plan B, C, or D. There is only what God ordained by his plan and our accountable actions. In his mysterious (to us) sovereignty, both of those become one.

Christ offers that unimaginable security to anyone who wants it enough to come to him for salvation. It is (to the self-sufficient mind) "too good to be true" that Christ could offer election to any creature who wanted it. He can offer God's chosen, personal love from eternity past to eternity future to those who come to him for it. Perhaps the gospel is the one thing in the universe that really is "too good to be true" but is. Again, no one has the faintest idea of how God does this, but he does. We can only gasp at the magnitude and sophistication of the way he shows his mercy and power.

Toxic Knowledge?

You may be like me during my first months in seminary. I resented and depreciated the idea that I was not in a position to understand God's governance of good and evil. I demanded, "How can you believe in the God of the Bible without having this level of knowledge? How do you even know Christianity is true without being able to check this out yourself?" Many have longed to know as God knows. I *demanded* to know.

That was the temptation of Adam and Eve in the Garden (Gen. 3:5). But it is the essence of God's power and strength that enables him to ordain and know every future event in heaven and in the cosmos. Such future knowledge is not given to us *for our own good.* There are a number of reasons why we would have trouble with such knowledge.

First, God's knowledge is exhaustive. It creates and covers the movement of every atomic particle since the dawn of creation. David even confessed that God's thoughts toward him are more than the sand of the seashore (Ps. 139:17). There are hundreds of millions of them. In short, God's plan by which he governs our world is way out of our league—both in sophistication and quantity of information. God could not, for instance, describe the ordinary way in which gravity and quantum theory relate and have even one scientist on earth understand it. Even the words *gravity* and *quantum* could be horribly superficial and not at all useful. Our knowledge even of the processes he has made evident is laughably primitive. For example, scientists have studied the simplest forms of life for a hundred years, and even though we have many samples of "primitive" life, we have not yet been able to generate even the simplest life form. God's questions to Job about nature (Job 38–42) challenged him to the point that Job insisted that God stop asking them.

We might, however, ask whether we could at least get a peek at the broad outlines of God's plan for our lives. That leads us to the second reason why we cannot know the plan of God. The information would damage us. It is too toxic for us to handle. Let me explain.

We might, for example, think it would be reassuring to see the list of those chosen by God for eternal life. Obviously, we would want to make sure we were among them. Or confirm that we missed the list so we could stop trying, relax, eat, drink, and be merry with the time remaining. But knowing with the certainty of God's knowledge that we would be saved no matter what we did or believed would corrupt us beyond recognition as Christians. That knowledge would be toxic to our Christian walk.

In counseling I have witnessed a couple of Christians who pitifully tried to blaspheme the Holy Spirit in order to seal their damnation. Such was their obsession to "know for sure." That way, they thought, they could at least have some control over their future and where they would spend eternity. They believed they could usurp God's control over the future. They concluded rightly that they could never know with the certainty of God whether they were going to heaven or hell. But they schemed that if they blasphemed the Holy Spirit, they (with God-like power) could thus decide their fate and find peace from uncertainty and anxiety. They lusted for the certainty of God's knowledge of the future—and were willing to trade their souls for it!

The knowledge of our death is another example of toxic knowledge. We might think it would be interesting to know the day and manner of our death, or the death of our children and loved ones. We naturally think it would be helpful to know the horrible things and the wonderful things that are going to happen years before they occur. Would it not be reassuring to know for sure whether our career would work out or not? Whether we would be a success at what we were attempting? Actually, when we think about it, the obvious comes to mind. If we had known what was involved in most of the things we did, we would never have started. We can handle the problems on a daily basis, but we could never handle them if we knew them all in advance.

The knowledge of good and evil is restricted to us by God's own love for us. The good is too good and the evil is too evil. He, for example, did not expose the origins of evil to Job, a godly and upright man who feared God in all the right ways. Neither did God tell Job about the cosmic battle between himself and Satan taking place through Job's sufferings. Similarly, God does not reveal his decretive plans to his creatures—and it is for our good.

The problem of evil has vexed Christians (particularly second generation Christians) for centuries. Non-Christians blithely brush off the claims of Christ by saying, "If God is so good and also sovereign, then why did he allow evil?" Of course, since God did not reveal the specific answer to that question, we have to tell them that. To nonbelievers that means automatically that either God is not good or not sovereign—or that he is neither. They instinctively restrict God's options to the ones they can imagine. That consists of what they can understand, with man's knowledge posited as the final, self-justifying, starting point for truth.

It never occurs to them that God is protecting us from information we are not able to handle. One day, I believe we will learn more about Satan's rebellion against God prior to the creation. We will learn more of the circumstances of Satan's creation. We will perhaps learn more about why God chose to save the world corrupted by Satan's influence, rather than wiping it out and beginning again. There may be levels of irrationality to the origin of evil that cannot be comprehended by finite creatures or that would be paralyzing if we were exposed to them now. We are in a position where we must be dependent on the good judgment of the Father who loves us and is determined to give us life despite our rebellion against him.

God has determined that, with some exceptions, the names of the elect and the lost must stay secret. The Book of Life and the other "books" are not opened until the Judgment Day (Rev. 20:12). The ultimate battle between good and evil, and the reflections of that battle in the providence of God, are best left to God.

Jesus teaches that we are "wired" to handle each day's anxiety each day—no more (Matt. 6:34). In my counseling practice I find that almost all anxiety-related problems are caused by a supposed need to know the future in some form. That is the appeal of astrologers, seers, witches, and the entire panoply of occult religionists. All that stands in stark contrast to the man who fears the Lord and therefore counts God equal to the task of governing the universe on his own.

"The knowledge of good and evil," in the limited way we understand it now, was a result of the rebellion of man against God (Gen. 3:5). Humanity wanted to know and understand the basis for everything God had commanded, but since we are not God, this knowledge created life-threatening problems for us. There seems to be an experiential component to knowing evil that is lethal. Even what God does reveal seems to be described in metaphorical language and leaves us with questions perhaps God consciously meant, for our own benefit, not to answer.

Moses beautifully states the distinction between the two kinds of knowledge in Deuteronomy 29:29.

> *The secret things belong to the LORD our God, but the things revealed belong to us and to our children forever, that we may follow all the words of this law.*

In this passage Moses teaches us to adjust to the idea of not knowing the secret things of God. Instead, he urges us to focus on what God *has* revealed, namely, the words of his law and how we may implement them today. He exhorts us not to waste time and energy seeking a way to unlock the secret plans of God, for ourselves or anyone else. God wants us to trust him for that. God desires us to focus on ordering our lives by what he has revealed—namely his Word.

Most occult knowledge centers on finding ways of penetrating the beneficial boundaries God has erected to our knowledge. Witches offer communication with the dead. The clairvoyant seek to penetrate the barriers between the minds of the living. Such practitioners do not trust God with their future or their finitude. They desire knowledge to give them power and relieve the anxiety resulting from their unbelief. In fact, Bruce Waltke argues that the notion of "finding the will of God" is pagan (Waltke 1995, 30) because it usually seeks to penetrate to the secret (decretive) plan of God.

Obtaining such direction from the gods was a major enterprise in most pre-Christian societies. It consumed a large portion of the time and money of the practitioners of non-Christian religions (Waltke 1995, 30). This power over future earthly life was also the primary supposed benefit. This benefit has been sought from the interior of Africa (Oosthuizen et al. 1988, 47–62) to the developed culture of the Druids (Ellis 1994, 248).

In contrast to knowledge that would promise man independence from God, Jesus revealed God in a nontoxic, nonlethal, and life-giving form. He told us what we needed to know to be reconciled with God and have a new life in him. His death on the cross changed our fearful and arrogant hearts so that we are able to be joyful creatures and not frustrated gods. We can now trust the God who controls our future and concentrate on living for him in the present.

It is a very liberating experience to have the crushing burden of the future removed from one's shoulders. Jesus did not come to give us access to the secret things of God's providence, but to reveal the hidden mystery of how God would redeem the fallen world. He gives us the truth that sets us free. His truth focuses our energy on present obedience and service. We can then say with Solomon, "In all your ways acknowledge him, and he will make your paths straight" (Prov. 3:6). God promises to take care of the obstacles in the paths of those who trust him. Jesus promises, "But seek first his kingdom and his righteousness, and all these things [our future needs] will be given to you as well" (Matt. 6:33). We can now return to Rick's situation with these truths in mind.

As Rick struggles to decide whether or not to go independent, he will not be able to discern the plan of God for him in advance. He can know, however, that because of the work of Christ, he is not on a permanent Plan B, C, or Z. In Christ there is only one plan: Plan A. He must do the hard work of finding biblical principles and values that apply to his situation. He must gather information on himself and his situation. He must pray and then make the decision. Rick can be greatly strengthened to know that he makes his decision in a protected environment. The Great Shepherd of the Sheep, the Almighty God, watches over him. That watch-care is called providence.

The Guardrail of Providence

God's providence is a bit like a guardrail on a mountain highway. Let me illustrate. One summer during my college years I traveled to South America on a missions trip with twelve other college-age musicians. One day we had to travel between two Colombian cities high in the Andes Mountains. We left at six in the morning and traveled until six that evening over a one-lane gravel road. This terrifying road was usually thousands of feet above the valley floor, with hairpin turns and switchbacks every few minutes.

There were no guardrails—*none!* I remember the driver barreling ahead with his horn blasting as we rounded each turn to warn some poor oncoming motorist that we were about to smash into him. Along the road there were little memorials to those who had gone over the sides. There were literally scores of these little flowered remembrances along the way. Because the bus held forty-two and there were sixty-five on board, I was privileged to stand up all day, which helped tremendously when I had to lean over three people to vomit out the window because I was carsick.

At any rate, at one point I was keenly aware of the fact that there really *was* a guardrail beside that road. It was the sovereign providence of God. I was actually comforted by the fact of my invincibility unless God himself gave his approval to our death by avalanche. I imagined an invisible and impenetrable guardrail, sustained and maintained by the living God. Incidentally, I thought we actually hit that invisible rail a number of times.

God's sovereign providence is like that guardrail to our decision making. We are hurtling down the mountain of life with turns and switchbacks constantly confronting us. Yet we can have confidence that God has established the boundaries of our lives. He holds us carefully in his hand despite the dangers we face and the foolish decisions we make. Only in heaven will we know the number of times we bumped into the guardrail of God's plan and were protected for his gracious purpose.

How can we not bow down and worship such a sovereign God, who cares for both the detailed and the huge issues of our lives? He is a God who protects us, trains us with his providential care, and loves us enough to teach us to trust him where it would be harmful for us to understand. Shouldn't the knowledge that there is such a sovereign plan work in us an attitude of worship, reverence, gratefulness, and confidence in the face of a world that appears out of control?

Those who are in Christ know that despite all the decisions we face, the mistakes we make, the sins we repent of, and the things we did not anticipate, God works in all things for the good of transforming us into the image of Christ, the Son of God (Rom. 8:28). Through his providence toward his children, God our Great Shepherd leads us by his mighty staff toward eternal life. If that is your goal in life, you are in very good hands!

For Review and Reflection

1. What is the crucial difference between the decretive will of God and the preceptive will?

2. How does confusing the two create impossible problems for the Christian facing life choices?

3. How do we reconcile God's sovereign control over all of life with our own moral responsibility?

4. Why doesn't God answer our questions about the problem of evil?

5. Why should our knowledge of God's sovereignty lead us to worship and trust him?

GUIDANCE AND THE
WORD OF GOD

IF God does not normally guide by giving us access to his sovereign plan, how *does* he provide direction? He gives us his words in Scripture. There his will is revealed in human language, and I hope to show that there alone we look for any real divine guidance.

In the previous chapter we reviewed the rich teaching of Scripture regarding the "will of God" in the sense of his secret, sovereign will and plan. We saw that the phrase "will of God" is also used in a second way in Scripture to mean the revealed truth and commandments of God. This is the "will of God" in the sense of what God desires or wants to happen, and this will be our focus in this chapter.

The Will of God: His Commandments

As we have said, this second usage of the phrase "the will of God" refers to God's commandments or precepts. For example, Matthew 6:10 records Jesus' teaching us to pray, "Your will be done on earth as it is in heaven." We can be sure that Jesus was not concerned that God's sovereign plans would fail unless people prayed. No, he was asking God to work so that men and women would obey his commandments here on earth, just as angels and heavenly beings obey them in heaven. Thus the phrase "will of God" is being used here in a moral sense, and Christ uses the phrase this way in many other portions of Scripture (Matt. 7:21; 12:50; Luke 11:2; 12:47; John 5:30, etc.).

In 1 Thessalonians 4:3, Paul writes, "It is *God's will* that you should be sanctified: that you should avoid sexual immorality." Paul is not predicting that the church would be pure in the providence of God. No, he is urging the believers there to seek holiness and sexual purity. The apostle Peter uses the same phrase when he declares, "For *it is God's will* that by doing good you should silence the ignorant talk of foolish men" (1 Peter 2:15). Clearly in both instances, the Bible is referring to God's will as what he commands for human beings, not what he ordains to happen. In some passages, both meanings apply at the same time. These passages refer both to (1) God's commanding a person to undertake a particular ministry and (2) his telling them the future of their work. Paul, for instance, often begins his letters stating that he is an apostle "according to the will of God" (1 Cor. 1:1; 2 Cor. 1:1; Eph. 1:1; Col. 1:1; etc.). In these cases both meanings apply because Christ appeared to Paul and, through Ananias (Acts 9:15), told him that he was his "chosen instrument" to carry Christ's name to the Gentiles. God pulled back the curtain on his eternal sovereign plan and let Ananias and Paul see some of it. Yet God's moral will was also involved because the Holy Spirit "called" (that is, commanded) Paul to take up his apostolic office (Acts 13:3).

This combined usage occurs in many of Jesus' teachings because he had access to much of God's plan as well as a deep knowledge of his commandments. He says in John 4:34, "My food is to do the will of him who sent me and to finish his work." God gave Jesus the task of coming to earth to die for our sin. Jesus was fully aware of this and in this verse was consciously submitting himself to it. It was both God's plan and command at the same time.

One day, in the new heavens and the new earth, that will be our experience as well. In fact, the convergence of these two "wills of God" is the very definition of heaven! There, what actually happens (providence) is also completely what God desires (his commands).

Now, however, we live in a fallen world. The will of God, as it refers to his plan, can contain many things that are contrary to the will of God as it refers to his commandment. For instance, God's sovereign plan included the fall into sin by Adam and Eve, the great flood in Noah's time, and the death of Christ. In this sense, even our sins are within the plan of God, yet he causes none of them.

You can see why it is so important that when we read about the will of God in Scripture, we understand the way or ways the phrase is used. The context makes it clear in all the relevant passages. With that distinction in mind, we can now look at how the will of God is revealed in the Bible.

The Sufficiency of Scripture

John 15 and 16 serve as a powerful springboard for our study. There, Jesus' teaching on the vine and the branches (John 15:1–17) has profound implications for our view of God's guidance. In this illustration, the vine represents Jesus; his Father is the gardener. The Father prunes back the good branches (believers) so that they provide more fruit. Branches that are attached to the vine but receive none of the life of the vine are dead. They are cut off and burned by the gardener.

Jesus teaches his listeners that they must be vitally united to him to produce life and fruit. He reminds them that despite the trauma of pruning (suffering and loss), his life shall not fail to bring about a fruitful result in their lives.

He also warns those who think they are attached to the vine to continually draw their life from it, that is, to "remain" in him. How often we fail to remain in Christ but try to attach ourselves to other false sources of life (our own righteousness, success, affection, esteem, security, or control, etc.)! He finishes the section by saying that all true (pruned) disciples bear fruit, marking themselves as God's.

Jesus Told Us Everything!

Jesus then addresses the question that interests us: How does God reveal his will? Note particularly verse 15. He says:

> [9] *As the Father has loved me, so have I loved you. Now remain in my love. [10] If you obey my commands, you will remain in my love, just as I have obeyed my Father's commands and remain in his love. [11] I have told you this so that my joy may be in you and that your joy may be complete. [12] My command is this: Love each other as I have loved you. [13] Greater love has no one than this, that he lay down his life for his friends. [14] You are my friends if you do what I command. [15] I no longer call you servants, because a servant does not know his master's business. Instead, I have called you friends, for everything that I learned from my Father I have made known to you. [16] You did not choose me, but I chose you to go and bear fruit—fruit that will last. Then the Father will give you whatever you ask in my name. [17] This is my command: Love each other.*

Verse 15 makes one of the most amazing statements in all of Scripture. Jesus says that he no longer calls his disciples "servants" but "friends." Jesus is making the distinction between the household servant who just follows orders and the true friend who is invited to enjoy the deepest sharing of heart with the owner of the house. A servant does not understand his master's deepest thoughts; he simply obeys instructions. Not so the friend. To the friend, the owner of the home discloses everything.

Let me illustrate. I am in the middle of renovating our basement area into a small "in-law" apartment. I hired a plumber to install a new heating system. When this man came to do the work, he never asked who was going to live there; he was not there as a friend but as a servant. He knew nothing of my short-term plans to allow my daughter to live there while she attended graduate school. Neither did he know of long-term possibilities for an elderly parent to use the quarters. But our close friends got the full story, complete with our deep concerns about our parents. I held nothing back; in return I got good advice and brotherly support.

It appears that Jesus is making this kind of sharp contrast here. He unveils a distinction between the way God's people related to God in the Old Testament era and the new way introduced by Christ with the gift of the Spirit.

The most challenging statement in the verse is, "Everything I learned from my Father I have made known to you." What in the world does Jesus mean by that? I believe he means what he says— *everything!* When you check the Greek, it means the same thing— *everything!* Everything in the vine is shared with the branches. The life and knowledge of one is completely offered to the other.

Jesus is intimately acquainted with the Father both as a man (in his human nature) and as the Son of God (in his divine nature). He studied the Scriptures without the moral blinders of sin. He astounded the temple elders with his insight. He underwent discipline and learned obedience by the things he suffered. He had discernment into the law of God that penetrated to the heart of every situation. He was full of wisdom and grace. Yet this statement goes beyond what Jesus knew in his human nature.

There are grounds to believe that Jesus is including in this statement everything he knew as the divine Son of God. When the Pharisees questioned Jesus, he said, "I have much to say in judgment of you. But he who sent me is reliable, and what I have heard from him I tell the world" (John 8:26). It appears that Jesus heard these things from his Father before becoming a man. In John 8:38, Jesus tells the Jews who believe in him, "I am telling you what I have seen in the Father's presence." He tells them that Abraham rejoiced to see his day (v. 56) and that "before Abraham was, I AM" (v. 58 NKJV). Jesus is a firsthand witness to what took place before he came into the world. He is reporting his experience as the divine Son of God. He goes on in John 12:49–50 to confirm this theme.

> *For I did not speak of my own accord, but the Father who sent me commanded me what to say and how to say it. I know that his command leads to eternal life. So whatever I say is just what the Father has told me to say.*

It is amazing that Jesus is not simply announcing that his disciples may listen in on his conversations with his Father, but that they can know everything he ever learned from him! That is the true and final friendship with God. This far surpassed anything Abraham (Isa. 41:8; James 2:23), Moses (Ex. 33:11), or David (1 Sam. 13:14) knew—though each of them was given access to God as a friend. Assuming that we understand this claim of Jesus, when and how do we go about enjoying this knowledge? The answer is given by Jesus in John 16.

Jesus goes on in John 15:16 to disclose another amazing implication of their position as "friends." He chose them to go and bear fruit that will last beyond death, fruit that will be a testimony to God's work in them throughout eternity.

Then he adds, "Then the Father will give you whatever you ask in my name." This is a summary of a point he made in verses 7–8. He says, in effect, as you abide in me and my words abide in you, God himself will grant your requests. As God's goals become your goals, you will find him answering your prayers. Prayers motivated by love for God's purposes will be answered. That is why Jesus ends the passage with a repeat of the command, "This is my command: Love one another" (v. 17).

In John 15:26, Jesus returns to the topic of the knowledge he has promised his disciples. He makes it clear that this knowledge from the Father comes in two stages or installments. He says, referring to stage two, "When the Counselor comes, whom I will send to you from the Father, the Spirit of truth who goes out from the Father, he will testify about me." Then in 16:12 he announces, "I have much more to say to you, more than you can now bear. But when he, the Spirit of truth, comes, he will guide you into all truth."

Jesus had been teaching his disciples intensively for three years. The sheer power and majesty of what he had revealed about himself, the Father, the Spirit, the coming new age, the unbelief of the Jewish people, and his own death were, to say the least, monumental. That is what we are calling installment one. Yet there was much more to be said—far more than they could yet assimilate. For that, they were to wait for the coming of the Spirit. He would guide them into "all the truth." The Holy Spirit would continue Jesus' teaching ministry until he had revealed everything that Jesus had learned from the Father.

Jesus confirms this interpretation in the next verse where he declares, "He [the Spirit] will not speak on his own; he will speak only what he hears, and he will tell you what is yet to come. He will bring glory to me by taking from what is mine and making it known to you. All that belongs to the Father is mine. That is why I said the Spirit will take from what is mine and make it known to you" (John 16:13–15). God has given all knowledge to Jesus; Jesus sends the Spirit to give it to his disciples, to equip them with everything Jesus had so that they can relate directly to the Father, as did Jesus (see vv. 19–27).

Jesus was aware that the words he gave the apostles were the very words of God. He was also confident that the words the Spirit would give (when they were ready) would also be the words of God, the continuation of his ministry. What Jesus is promising is nothing less than a new revelation, an addition to the Word of God (the Old Testament Scriptures) beyond what he taught in his earthly ministry. It would complete the revelation of the Father.

There was an intense period of some forty years when the Spirit of God spoke through the apostles in order to witness to and interpret the death and resurrection of Christ. This process completed the revelation Christ promised in John 15:15. The church was established on the "Rock" of the apostles' confessing what the Spirit revealed (Matt. 16:15–18).[1]

This ministry was largely completed by the end of the apostolic era (about A.D. 100) when all the apostles had died, as well as most of those specially commissioned to extend and represent their ministry (Timothy, Titus, John Mark, etc.). At this point in the development of the church, the leadership passed to "those who believed through their [the apostles'] message" (John 17:20).

Our confidence that the particular books of the Bible are the right ones rests on Jesus' promise to reveal everything through the apostles for those who believe through their message. These particular books complete the testimony to the Father that Jesus began (Matt. 16:18; Rev. 22:18–19). Jesus did build the church on the foundation of the

---

1 See Edmund Clowney's masterful discussion of this text in *The Church,* page 73. He shows that the apostle Peter by himself was not the "rock" (as traditional Catholic theology holds), nor was Peter's confession by itself the "rock" (as traditional Protestant theology holds). Rather, Clowney points out that Matthew 16:13–20 teaches that it is the apostle confessing what the Spirit reveals that forms the "rock" upon which Christ builds the church. See also Eph. 2:20 and 1 Cor. 3:10–11.

"apostles confessing what the Spirit revealed." He promised it, and our confidence in these books must rest ultimately on the confidence we place in Jesus—not on how well we can prove the authenticity or special miraculous quality of each book by some external measure, such as proven apostolic authorship or extremely early dating of the book.

Confirmed in the Epistles

The epistles give us the same picture of the way in which the Father gave his full revelation to the church. In Ephesians 2:20 Paul sought to describe the Gentiles' place in the church with a word picture of the church as a building. He says, "Consequently, you are no longer foreigners and aliens, but fellow citizens with God's people and members of God's household, *built on the foundation of the apostles and prophets*" (Eph. 2:19–20). He uses the same imagery in 1 Corinthians 3:10–11 when he says,

> *By the grace God has given me, I laid a foundation as an expert builder, and someone else is building on it. But each one should be careful how he builds. For no one can lay any foundation other than the one already laid, which is Jesus Christ.*

Again, Paul pictures the church as resting on a foundation he laid as the master builder. This time, he calls Jesus Christ that foundation. Notice what these two passages are saying. The terms "Jesus Christ" and "apostles and prophets" are interchangeable in this context because Christ uses the apostles and prophets as if he himself were speaking. The key distinction is between the foundation (laid once for all by Christ, the apostles, and prophets) and those who must build upon it (we who come later, who believe through their message).

Paul is very conscious that he is fulfilling Jesus' promise to build the church on the rock of the apostles and prophets. He sees himself and the other apostles revealing that "second installment" of the Father's truth, which is nothing less than the completion of Jesus' revelation. Paul could tell his young understudy Timothy that all Scriptures are "God-breathed . . . that the man of God may be thoroughly equipped for every good work" (2 Tim. 3:16). Peter reflects the same confidence in the completeness and sufficiency of Scripture in 2 Peter 1:3. He declares, "His divine power has given us everything we need for life and godliness through our knowledge of him who called us by his own glory and goodness."

I hope you sense the powerful message from Christ: that his Word (the Bible) is complete, sufficient, and thoroughly powerful for the completion of the faith and life of every child of God.

Can you see the revolutionary implications of Jesus' promise to tell his disciples everything he had learned from his Father? In his earthly ministry and the ministry of his apostles and prophets, Jesus fully granted us that truth. Everything he knows as the Son of God he has given us to know. And despite our sin, the power of the Holy Spirit opens our hearts to hear it, believe it, and do it—not perfectly, but substantially and visibly.[2]

Such teaching obviously closes the door on supposed "revelations" that are additions to the Bible. This is common to heretical cults, such as the Watchtower Society and the Mormon religion. The completeness of revelation through Christ and the apostles makes it clear that we should not expect additional truths from the mind of God to us. In other words, revelation is as complete as Christ's atonement for sins!

Any claims for prophetic messages today must be stringently ex-

2 The Spirit also works to open people's hearts and minds to believe the Word he gave through the apostles. Even in apostolic times, this work of illumination by the Holy Spirit was the most important work (1 John 2:26–27; 1 Cor. 2:6–16). Illumination enables a blind sinner to see and understand the things of God. Revelation is the giving of the inspired words of God to man in human language.

amined in the light of this truth. Jonathan Edwards, the father of the Great Awakening, called the possibility of new revelations "the error that will support all errors" (Winship 1996, 150).

Whatever one's position on charismatic gifts, all would agree that the real challenge is for believers to mine the unsearchable riches of wisdom and knowledge hidden in Christ—but available to those who seek the full riches in Scripture. Paul sums it up well in Colossians 2:2–3, where he describes the purpose of his labor for the Colossians.

> *My purpose is that they may be encouraged in heart and united in love, so that they may have the full riches of complete understanding, in order that they may know the mystery of God, namely, Christ, in whom are hidden all the treasures of wisdom and knowledge.*

Notice the universal claims that Paul makes for the results of apostolic ministry: that they may have the full riches of complete understanding in Christ, in whom are *all* the treasures of wisdom and knowledge.

There are good grounds, then, for believing that the Scriptures provide all the wisdom and knowledge we need from God. Our blindness hides much of it from our eyes, but that does not mean that we should "dumb down" our expectations from Scripture so that they match our blindness. Rather, we should open our eyes to learn of this wisdom, expecting the revelation of the mind of Christ to provide the key to any wisdom we may seek from God.

The Bible or the Bible Plus?

The purpose of this book is to show how God uses the Bible to guide his children through this life. Everyone who writes from any Christian perspective teaches that Scripture is the primary way in which God reveals his will. Most of those same writers, however, go on to add other ways in which God reveals his preferences and desires for believers. To confine oneself to the Holy Spirit speaking through Scripture seems limiting at first in the face of the highly specific questions we face in our lives. In the case of Rick we think, *He surely won't be able to find out whether to start his own business by reading the Bible!*

Sensing this limitation, some teach that in addition to Scripture (but not in contradiction to it), God reveals the specifics of his will through such things as vivid impressions, dreams, amazing circumstances, and a subjective sense of peace. We have all had these experiences. What are we to make of them? We shall look at the role these occurrences play and discover that they are works of God's providence, not revelations of God's will. We will explore this distinction in the chapters ahead, and shall see that they provide the *context* for God's guidance, though they do not make up that guidance themselves. Instead, I want to show that the Bible, properly understood and applied by the Holy Spirit, is completely sufficient for the guidance of the believer, even in today's world of minivans, HMOs, digital information, blended families, and enshrined secularism.

Applying the Bible to Guidance Issues

You may be thinking, *Of course the Bible is sufficient for moral guidance, for telling the difference between right and wrong. But how does it help me know whether to take a particular job? How does it help me know whether to go to graduate school or support my friend's plans to marry an older man?*

When we need guidance, it usually involves a situation in which the basic alternatives are all legitimate—legally and biblically. Most people who seek to be obedient Christians are not puzzled over what is prohibited in Scripture. That is, we are not struggling to know whether God would want us to take his name in vain, commit adultery, or practice fraud. But we do have questions about the positive things that are commanded, like love your neighbor, wife, child, brother, enemy, etc.

Three years ago I gathered a group of my friends together to advise me regarding the development of my ministry. I had distilled five possible directions for my future work and, despite praying for wisdom, I was having a difficult time eliminating four of them and choosing one. Each of the five options was biblically permissible. None was sin in itself, but not all were equally appropriate for me at this time in my life. Interestingly, even my friends did not agree on which one was most fitting, but their questions eventually helped me narrow the field to one option.

Most questions of guidance are these kinds of questions—questions like the ones we listed in chapter 1. They require going much deeper than asking whether the options are sinful in themselves. There are often profound spiritual issues at stake in decisions between intrinsically lawful alternatives.

Luke 10:25–37 is an example of this. Jesus relates the parable of the "good Samaritan" and describes the behavior of the priest and the Levite. They walk right past the seriously wounded victim, moving away from him so as not to confront his pleas. The priest and the Levite were perhaps on their way to perform an important religious duty, and the wounded man could have been bait for another robbery attempt. Yet Jesus makes it clear that they did not show biblical mercy and thus failed to be a true neighbor. Now, there is no specific law in the Old Testament that required them to stop and help all robbery victims. Yet they violated the moral will of God by not stopping.

We are faced with similar situations every day as we drive down the highways and see stranded motorists. There is no biblical law that says we must stop and help at a given moment. And there are many other factors that we must take into consideration (our spouse's reaction if we are late, our responsibility for safety, our son's need for help with his homework, etc.). Yet Jesus did teach us to "do to others what you would have them do to you" (Matt. 7:12).

This principle fulfills "all the law and the prophets," according to Jesus. Guidance seeks to apply this great commandment along with many goals, values, and directions that follow from it. Divine guidance, then, illuminates our minds to apply all these things to the vast array of lawful choices confronting us in life.

God's guidance helps us to discern the best and right among choices that qualify as lawful (i.e., not prohibited in Scripture). This requires setting priorities among absolutes. Let me explain. God commands us to evangelize, do missions, remember the poor, exhort and encourage one another, worship publicly and privately, visit the prisoner, show hospitality, love our spouses, bring up our children, and work at our vocation with all our heart. The question, as John Frame points out, is not *whether* we do them, but *when,* and *in what order* (Frame 1991, 115). Frame rightly recognizes that for the positive commands of Scripture, God calls us to "prioritize among absolutes." We cannot do them all at once. We must choose when a particular positive act is a priority and when it is not. Each of us must therefore develop a sense of priorities reflecting our gifts, our situation, and our callings, and our goals to glorify God. These are the issues that constitute the real battleground of guidance. This is where we seek to know and do the will of God.

As each of us applies the great commandments to our own individual circumstances, our own unique path will emerge. Our calling will develop, and our work and ministry will be embodied. There we will find our path—following Christ's steps, yet taking our own.

For Review and Reflection

1. In what sense is the will of God not secret, but intended for us to know? In what sense is it secret?

2. What do you think Jesus meant when he promised to reveal to us "everything the Father had shown him" (John 15:14–15)?

3. How did Jesus fulfill that promise? Do you think he has completed it today?

4. Was there a unique role for the apostles and prophets in the New Testament church age? How would you describe it?

5. Do you believe that there is more that God wanted to reveal to the church after the first generation of the apostles and prophets? What is your basis for that belief?

6. In what ways can the Bible help us with decisions about circumstances it does not specifically mention?

CHAPTER

Guidance and the "Individual Will of God"

THE individuality of our callings brings us to the next question: Does God have an "individual will" for each of us—a will that is different from his secret, sovereign plan and yet also different from his clearly revealed commandments? We tend to refer loosely to "knowing God's will for our life." A couple might, for instance, ask whether it was God's will for them to adopt a child rather than bear natural children. *Is* there an individual, ideal plan that God has for us, separate from his commands?

For example, would God have a preference as to whether Rick should begin his own graphic design company or remain an employee? God may well have such a preference for what is best for Rick; one choice may be more consistent with the commandment to love as we have been loved. So far so good. The problems come when Rick thinks about God's preferences as if they are somehow disconnected from his commands, his values, or his Word. Rick is in trouble if he thinks that getting guidance from God is like getting a peek at the map of his life—an ideal pattern God has planned for him.

In popular Christian teaching this "will of God" is sometimes identified as "God's perfect will" or the "center of God's will" or God's "specific will." In evangelical circles, it is still usually used in this sense of a heavenly map for our lives that covers nonmoral specifics. It assumes that there is a will of God that is separate and distinct from God's sovereign will, yet is something beyond his moral will or commandments. Typically it is thought to cover decision making in areas of employment, marriage, finances, lifestyle, and ministry.

Gary Maeder illustrates this perspective well.

> I believe that God has an individual will for all Christians on some matters. For me that would clearly seem to include my involvement with the deputation program of the First Presbyterian Church of Hollywood, my seminary studies, my marriage, my legal career and our children. Quite possibly it includes much more. In each of these areas, discovering and carrying out God's will for my life meant seeking and making the specific choice He desired for me. For other believers, God's individual will would involve different decisions and events. (Maeder 1973, 14)

Maeder seems to be saying that there are important events in the life of every believer for which God has a specific will. This will must be discovered by the believer not by an application of scriptural values to the decision, but by some other means. Maeder insists that such means be consistent with Scripture.

At first it may seem that the differences here are primarily semantic. But closer examination shows that they involve two incompatible principles of guidance. Maeder's view assumes that God has a third kind of will—his individual will—which believers should ask him to reveal. I believe, however, that there are only two uses of the phrase "will of God" in Scripture.

Garry Friesen has done an excellent study on whether there is such a thing as a personal will of God. He has also provided a definition of this popular notion (Friesen 1980, 35): "God's Individual will is that ideal, detailed life-plan which God has uniquely designed for each believer." This plan is not contained in Scripture either explicitly or implicitly.

Friesen rightly points out that this view underlies the "Bull's eye" theory of the will of God. He uses the picture of a target to show how the moral will relates to the individual will of God. God's moral will is seen as a circular target. Our decisions are like arrows we shoot at the target, seeking to hit God's will. Inside the circle are all the lawful choices. Outside the target are all options that are always sinful. If you miss the target, your decision is sin against God and contradicts the moral law.

The individual will of God is seen as the bull's eye on the target. That is the "will" we seek to discover (hit) for guidance. If we miss the bull's eye but hit within the target area, we are not in sin—but we *are* missing God's best for us. We have made a wrong turn on God's map for our lives. We are then said to be outside the individual will of God, but still within his moral will.

Rick's dilemma can illustrate this view. For purposes of illustration, let's suppose that God's "ideal" plan for Rick was to begin his own business. In this theory, if Rick chose to stay an employee, that decision would be considered outside the individual will of God but inside the moral will of God. Things might go wrong, but he would not be violating anything in Scripture. Nor should it disrupt his fellowship with God.

Four Problems

There are at least four problems with this conception of the individual will of God. The first is that by focusing on God's individual (nonmoral) will, Rick might be overlooking a sinful motive of his heart or an important application of a scriptural principle. For instance, if he stays an employee instead of starting his own business, he could be ignoring his gifts and seeking to serve only because of situational factors like money, security, and status. If he only focuses on whether or not his outward choice violates this "individual will of God," his inner motives will go unexplored. He will miss the spiritual insight involved in applying the positive commands of Scripture to his life and motives.

Second, the view improperly focuses Rick on discovering a plan rather than applying Scripture in the wisdom of the Spirit. Rick would focus on interpreting circumstances, looking for "signs" of God's direction, setting up tests to determine God's leading ("fleecing"), listening for inaudible voices or audible ones. Obviously, most of us would love God to send us a message telling us what to do. I am sure Rick wanted God to reveal the next intersection on the unseen map of his life and remove him from the decision-making process. Yet it is the process of developing insight, character, and wisdom that is most valuable to God. If God provided Rick with directions for the next intersection on his map, Rick would not have grown. As Rick struggles, consults, meditates, and prays, it becomes clearer that he must do a sober evaluation of his enterprising and management gifts, his motives, his financial responsibilities to his family, his wife's tolerance for risk and uncertainty, the trade-off between greater flexibility of hours against the longer hours he would have to put in. He will have to evaluate how those trade-offs will affect his devotional life, and church and family involvement. Only that kind of self-knowledge will yield a wise and godly decision.

The third problem is that this view is nowhere taught in Scripture. The phrase "will of God" is simply not used in this sense of an idealized personal plan that forms a pattern for decision making. This supposed "individual will" is not God's sovereign will, which is behind providence, nor is it the revealed will of God in Scripture. It is something in between these two and separate from them. The passages that are cited (Col. 1:9; 4:12; Rom. 12:2; Eph. 5:17; 6:6), all actually refer to God's will as revealed in his commandments and applied to our lives. So advocates of this view are using a category that is not introduced in Scripture—a big problem! Friesen has a very good analysis of each of these passages (Friesen 1980, 97–113).

A fourth difficulty with this concept is that it is unworkable. By that I mean that if there is an ideal personal plan for our lives, most of us have strayed far from it. That is definitely true for me just based on the number of decisions I've made that later proved to be wrong. Once a person takes a wrong turn on a map, he must return to the spot of the wrong turn and take the correct route. In life, of course, we cannot go back to previous decision points. Finding the way back after numerous wrong turns becomes nigh unto impossible.

"Missing" God's Best

Some attempts have been made to deal with this problem and reassure us that we should not worry if we have "missed" God's best. M. Blaine Smith tries to deal with this difficulty in his book *Finding God's Will*. He says,

> I can be free of the fear that a past decision made in faith may later be found to be outside of God's will. We may be convinced that a certain decision is in God's will, but later discover new information which would have caused us to decide differently, and we conclude that we must have misjudged God's leading. . . . If we take God's sovereignty in guidance seriously, we must conclude that such rehashing of past decisions is really unnecessary. It is also impious. (Smith 1991, 60)

It is interesting to note that Smith must leave the concept of the individual will and point to God's sovereign will in order to comfort someone worried about past departures from the individual will of God. Let's say, for instance, that a wife becomes convinced that she married outside the individual will of God (i.e., she was supposed to marry someone else in God's plan). Her husband is a Christian but has since neglected her for his Christian ministries. She can, of course, comfort herself in God's sovereign plan, but it will be difficult not to think about the man she was supposed to marry—as she serves the man who ignores her. It is a theology that cries out for speculation on what the ideal plan might have been—if only it had been followed. Smith rebukes such thinking as impious, but once the concept of an individual will is ingrained, it is hard to just forget about it when things go wrong. While we can heartily agree that God sovereignly uses everything together for good in the believer's life, this does not explain what happened to the divine road map from which the straying believer departed.

We are assured that God will still work with us where we are (down in Plan D, F, or Z) and that he will get us back to the key departure points of his sovereign plan (Smith 1991, 61). But it seems again that there is a tendency to offer the concept of an individual will with the right hand and take it back with the left. Kenneth Geiser illustrates this point as follows:

> God will bless you for every effort you put forth even if you feel you missed His main great pattern for your life. (Geiser 1968, 60)

While that sounds reassuring, I cannot find it in Scripture—except in appeal to the *sovereign* will of God. Writers in this vein point to the many biblical examples in which great saints have made horrible decisions, yet God has worked out his plan in their lives (Smith 1991, 61).

But Scripture explicitly explains this as the work of God's sovereign and gracious will working around and through human sin, not as an exception to an ideal personal plan.

Paul the apostle says, "Where sin increased, grace increased all the more" (Rom. 5:20). In fact, it is only by the knowledge of sin that we see our need of Christ, initially and on a daily basis. In that sense, Christ even redeems our sin. The lives of Adam, Moses, and David are marvelous illustrations of God sovereignly working—even through sin—his plan to bring salvation to the world and to these individuals.

The concept of an individual will separate from God's moral will is thus not scriptural. Despite its popularity, this concept should be rejected. What is often called the "individual will of God" should be seen simply as the application of God's commands and character to the specifics of our lives. It is not a separate and distinct (nonmoral) sense of God's will.

To sum up, God has a secret, sovereign plan for each of us that orders each detail of our lives. God also has a revealed, moral will for us that is summarized in the Great Commandment and has implications, preferences, and directions for extensive areas in each life. The wisdom we seek in divine guidance is God's moral will applied to the believer's life. Guidance is discerning God's moral and spiritual preferences as they apply to our life situations. It is not a detailed plan to be discovered or communicated by God in extra-scriptural communications.

Fleece and Other Tests for Guidance

Anxious Christians who do not understand this truth often end up resorting to the use of "fleece" (Judges 6:36–40) as a means of divining the will of God. In Judges 6, Gideon is commanded to lead a small Israelite army out to battle against a huge force of Midianites. Gideon did not believe God's call at first and so devised a test to which God would submit, thereby proving that he was calling Gideon to lead this battle. Gideon put out dry fleece (probably sheep wool) one night and asked that there be dew on everything in the morning, but that the fleece remain dry. The next night he put out another fleece and asked that there be dew on the fleece and that everything else be dry. God graciously submitted to both tests, and Gideon's weak faith was rallied.

Christians of weak faith often end up using such tests, together with a reliance on hunches, impressions, circumstances, intuitive senses, open doors, and other shaky methods for discerning the will of God. The fact that God gave signs and "fleece" because of the unbelief of Israel is testimony to his amazing patience, a patience he also exercises today with fearful believers.

The more difficult the decision (like the one Rick must make), the more dangerous it is to try to discern the extrabiblical clues we hope God might be dropping our way. Rick, in our story, finally realized that if God had a preference about his decision, it would be biblically based. He stopped asking God to tell him what to do, or to make the decision for him. Rather, Rick began earnestly to ask God for wisdom and self-understanding. He asked some friends to help him prayerfully evaluate his gifts and abilities, the potential effects of a change on his family (given the amount of money he had to start with), and priorities that might be affected in his life. He interviewed others who had gone independent, potential customers (since he did not have a non-compete clause in his current contract), and a banker who financed such ventures.

After a season of prayer, Rick made the decision to move into his own business. He became convicted that God had given him the gifts and motivations necessary to make such a start-up venture succeed. He believed that God wanted him to serve according to the way God had gifted and designed him (Rom. 12:3–8) and in the circumstances into which he had placed him.

To summarize then, divine guidance comes as we

➤ internalize and adopt God's values and commandments, and

➤ express them in our unique situation

➤ through the illumination of the Holy Spirit.

The Three Circles

While no diagram can exhaustively portray the relationship between God, his Word, and ourselves, another target diagram composed of three circles has helped many understand these basics (see Figure 1).

The concept of God's moral will can be visualized as three concentric circles. We will begin by discussing the two inner ones and discuss the third, outside circle (representing the area of Christian freedom) in the next chapter.

The inner circle represents all actions that are expressly prohibited in Scripture: Do not murder; do not worship idols; do not steal; do not gossip or slander. To do such prohibited things is clearly sin against

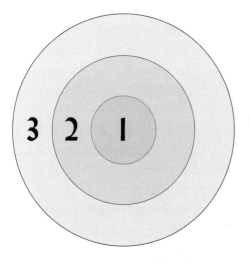

1. AREA OF THINGS PROHIBITED
   • "Put offs"
   • Requires obedience in all situations
   • Area of church discipline

2. AREA OF THE APPLICATION OF GOD'S POSITIVE COMMANDS
   • Guidance by wisdom and discernment
   • Can be in or out of God's will depending on the situation, motive, outcome, etc.

Figure 1. The three circles of God's will

God. Because such actions are always sin (no matter what the circumstances), the person who is continually unrepentant of them should be subject to church discipline. For example, it is never right to rob a bank, commit fornication, or cheat on your tax return. If a person commits such an act and does not repent, he should be disciplined by his church.

In the case of actions prohibited by God, we must refrain from *all* of these actions *all* the time. We do not prioritize among them or refrain from some but not others depending on the situation. That was the heresy of the "situation ethics" debate in the 1960s. It denied the moral absolutes of Scripture that are the foundation of Christian ethics.

A second, larger, concentric circle represents all the positive commands in Scripture, summarized in the Great Commandment. Most guidance questions arise within this circle. As we have seen, no one can keep all of these commands at once. We generally can do only one at a time. This means we must establish priorities among the commands, determining when each is called for.

For example, when I come home from work, I must choose whether to spend some time debriefing with my wife ("Husbands, love your wives") or answer an urgent phone call from a counselee ("Feed my sheep"). I cannot do both at once. If I try, I will just create problems on both fronts. On a longer term basis, I also make priority decisions about whether I will coach Little League ("Fathers, bring up your children . . . do not exasperate them") or join the building committee of the church ("Be steadfast, unmoved, always abounding in the work of the Lord"). If I can do both, I must decide when to do them. I may also have to decide between them if one is of significantly greater importance than the other. All of these forms of love are commanded by the Lord, but they require discernment and the setting of priorities regarding what we do and when.

This second circle of God's moral will covers areas just as critical to our moral and spiritual well-being as the inner circle of God's prohibitions. Garry Friesen sees this area as governed by the principle of "spiritual expediency," not morality (Friesen 1980, 151–281). Friesen has made an enormous contribution in exposing the unbiblical concept of the "individual will of God." However, while heading in the right direction, the term "spiritual expediency" needs to be greatly strengthened. In my view, this second circle is where believers work out all the positive commands of Scripture. There is more than "spiritual expediency" at stake here: the very heart of moral integrity is involved.

The positive commands of Scripture cover some of the most critical areas of our lives. We'll look next at several of them. As we do, ask yourself, "Are decisions in this area based on expediency or are they much more important?" Let's see.

Money

A casual look through 2 Corinthians 8–9 reveals the deep spiritual significance of generosity. Paul says, "Just as you excel in everything—in faith, in speech, in knowledge, in complete earnestness and in your love for us—see that you also excel in this grace of giving" (2 Cor. 8:7). God commands generosity, which makes it an intensely moral issue. Jesus says, "Where your treasure is, there will your heart be also." Money is an issue that goes to the heart of our relationship to God.

What does it mean to excel in the grace of giving? Paul did not set a dollar figure and then command the Corinthians to give it. He commanded generosity—which is different (but real) for each person. Instead of a dollar figure, he points them to Christ. "For you know the grace of our Lord Jesus Christ, that though he was rich, yet for your sakes he became poor, so that you through his poverty might become rich" (2 Cor. 8:9). Paul points them back to Jesus' simple commandment to love one another as we ourselves have been loved by God. He beautifully balances the command of generosity with the need for each believer to give out of the motive of gratefulness to Christ ("cheerfully," 2 Cor. 9:7) and according to the determination of his own heart.

In determining the amount that we give, we make decisions that reach into every corner of our lives. Our giving affects our sought-for standard of living, our sense of what makes us successful or secure, and our sense of generous provision for our children and their education.

Wisely, the church does not consider the dollar amounts of one's gifts an area where she should exercise church discipline. That clearly violates the freedom that Christ has purchased for us in the positive obedience we offer him. In the same way, the pattern of our spending reflects our heart's response to God, who entrusts us with money as his stewards. While it is an area of freedom before the church and others, it is not a question of expediency with God. It goes to our heart and its response to Christ. In that sense it is intensely moral and spiritual and requires spiritual eyes to see what one "ought" to do.

Giftedness

In addition to money, God had called us to be stewards of our abilities and gifts. This is another area that many believe to be spiritually neutral and pragmatically controlled. Yet in reality it also is intensely spiritual and moral. It is an area where we want to know the will of God; where we ask, "What does God want me to do for him?"

In Exodus God calls "all the skilled men to whom I have given wisdom in such matters" (Ex. 26:1, 31, 36; 28:2, 6, 11, 15, 39; 30:15) to undertake the construction of the tabernacle. He did not gift them just at the moment they were needed to build the tabernacle. They had been gifted earlier and were using their skills in the trades. God gave them wisdom in the construction trades and in craftsmanship while they were still slaves in Egypt. Almost certainly they worked on the projects of the Pharaoh.

In the same way God grants wisdom to each of us in particular matters, that we may serve him both in the world and in the church. We are recipients of the gifts and abilities given us by God and this is a matters of much more than pragmatic concern.

Romans 12:3–8 is a key passage. We have already looked at Romans 12:1–2, where Paul calls for the consecration of our entire lives and for a renewed mind, so that we might know by experience how excellent the will of God is. Paul applies that "living sacrifice" teaching in verse 3 by talking about our gifts. He says,

> *For by the grace given me I say to every one of you: Do not think of yourself more highly than you ought, but rather think of your-self with sober judgment, in accordance with the measure of faith God has given you. Just as each of us has one body with many members, and these members do not all have the same function, so in Christ we who are many form one body, and each member belongs to all the others. (Rom. 12:3–5)*

Paul appeals to the Roman Christians to develop not so much a *good* self-image as an *accurate* one.[1] This is to be done with sober judgment, avoiding the pitfalls of a deceived and overly exalted view of oneself. Paul then points to the "measure of faith" as the factor that should govern the way we think and act. We see from the context that this measure of faith is not faith for salvation but faith for the work God has called us to do. It is faith for ministry and service.

Paul is saying that our gifts and abilities are not sufficient in themselves to fulfill what God has called us to do. They must be exercised

---

1 John Bettler, class notes, June Institute of Counseling Studies, 1978.

in the confidence that God himself can work through them. Paul puts as much stock in our motivation for exercising our gift as he does in the sheer ability. Understanding the crucial role that motivation plays, he goes so far as to warn prophets not to prophesy beyond their "measure of faith" (Rom. 12:6). Though prophecy was a miraculous gift at that time in the church, Paul wanted it kept in tandem with confidence in God, not in the gift.

Paul makes it clear that faith must motivate the use of all the gifts listed in Romans 12: service, encouraging, contributing, leadership, and mercy—the nonmiraculous gifts and the miraculous ones. Believing that God can work through you despite your weaknesses and sins, and stepping out in faith to exercise that gift, is the key to Christian motivation. It grasps the vision that ministry is not one's own, but God's.

This principle is also taught by Peter in 1 Peter 4:10–12:

> *Each one should use whatever gift he has received to serve others, faithfully administering God's grace in its various forms. If anyone speaks, he should do it as one speaking the very words of God. If anyone serves, he should do it with the strength God provides, so that in all things God may be praised.*

Peter's point is the same as Paul's: the gifts of God can only be properly exercised in the confidence that God is at work in their use. That motivating faith must be discerned in the service of every Christian.

Discerning your gifts and your motivation for exercising them are important issues when you seek to do God's will in your work, both in the church and in your secular vocation. God assigns the gifts for service, and he gives each believer different ones. Therefore, God certainly has individual preferences for our individual ministries. He wants us to discover our gifts and ministry—not by looking into his secret plan, or by following clues to understand his ideal plan for our lives, but by exercising insight into our own design, and faith and wise judgment in our use of those abilities.

Some of us will discover this aspect of God's will fairly early and will reap some blessings as a result. Others will try to minister or work outside their giftedness and calling, and experience frustration. Sometimes that slowness of discernment can be caused by fear, pride, or plain foolishness (not listening). This I know by personal experience.

I remember that the conditions of my first call to ministry were horrible. Five students (myself included) had begun a church at the University of Pennsylvania while we were still in seminary. Three graduated and left the area the next year. The fourth did so one year later. By the time I graduated, I was the only one left. Since my wife and I have the ability to organize, we had been doing a lot of the behind-the-scenes work of the church. So instead of asking for a group to help me examine my gifts for pastoral ministry, I volunteered to lead the church and was duly called to the office.

I pastored for twelve years and God blessed it in a number of ways. However, it took me ten years to recognize that at that time I lacked some necessary gifts and faith for pastoral leadership. I learned much about myself and my strengths, and the stress that I experienced was used powerfully by God in my growth. In fact, it was the most powerful engine of spiritual growth I've had in my life.

In those situations, those who are slow to enter into their giftedness have only to repent, seek cleansing, and respond with new insight and obedience. There is no "life plan" that they have blown, any more than with any other sin they have committed or poor choice they have made. There is just the command of God: serve one another according to your gifts as the Lord has served you. Again, this may appear to be a nonmoral area, but it is actually one of deep spiritual significance, where discernment of God's will is mandated.

Chapter Six

Time

Time use is another area that might not seem to be governed by the specific, direct commands of God, except when it comes to observing the Sabbath (Ex. 20). Yet in the New Testament, we are urged to discover the will of God regarding time use—in the sense of what he wants or desires from us. A key passage is Ephesians 5:15–18.

> *Be very careful, then, how you live—not as unwise but as wise, making the most of every opportunity, because the days are evil. Therefore do not be foolish, but understand what the Lord's will is. Do not get drunk on wine, which leads to debauchery. Instead, be filled with the Spirit.*

Here Paul again emphasizes the importance of careful consideration, this time of the opportunities that God provides us in the time remaining before his return. He is not talking about time management skills in the usual sense. Rather, he calls for discernment of the priorities of godly living.

One implication of this passage is that time must be discerned and mastered. To use the literal language of the King James Version, it must be "redeemed" because the times (days) are evil. If we waste the opportunities God affords us by blindly pursuing our self-oriented, earthly purposes or just going with the flow, we will be the fool who "does not understand the will of God." Living for "that which is seen" submits us to the fallen natural order, and our lives will be without the formative fruitfulness of God's Spirit. Here again we see the connection between understanding the will of God and something that might not seem (at first glance) to be very moral or spiritual—the use of our opportunities with biblical priorities in view. (Romans 13:11–14 makes a similar point.) Let me illustrate.

Why did the priest and Levite in the parable of the Good Samaritan get it wrong? Their failure was not related to a lack of time to stop and help (though most time management systems would discourage such a "diversion" from personal goals). Their failure was rooted in their fundamental lack of mercy (Luke 10:37). Godly priorities in that situation were missed because of a self-oriented heart and outlook. They lived uncritically—lost in their own goals—and missed the will of God.

Knowing the will of God requires that we make priority decisions regarding all the relationships that Paul describes in Ephesians 5:18–6:17: church, marriage, parenting, work, and personal development. God wants all of those areas of life to be lived out under the control of the Spirit.

The life ruled by ("under the influence" of) the Holy Spirit is a life of multiple priorities. There are many positive callings to which we must respond each day. The passage above describes the core values for each of these important areas of life. Husbands, for example, must love and nourish their wives. Wives must respect and support the leadership of their husbands. Children must obey and honor their parents. Parents must bring their children up in the Lord, and so on. Paul continues in this vein through Ephesians 6:20. If we claim to have the Spirit-filled life, the fulfillment of these core values must be at the heart of our lifestyles, schedules, and commitments.

I have developed an exercise to help you gauge how you are doing at discerning and fulfilling the core priorities of your life. Here is how it works.[2] Make a list of each of the activities you believe you ought to do in a normal four-week period. Include every activity

2 I have included in the appendix directions, illustrations, and the forms necessary to complete the Assessing My Priorities Worksheet (AMP). Copies of the AMP can be obtained from Resources for Changing Lives, 1803 East Willow Grove Ave, Glenside, PA 19038, phone 1-800-318-2186.

under some category—sleep, work, transportation time, eating, resting, exercise, friends, relatives, spouse, children, church activities, etc. Next, assign the amount of time you believe it should actually take to do each of those activities properly during a four-week period. Add up the total time you believe you need for the four-week period to do all these things, and add 5 percent extra time to allow for the inefficiency of life. The results may surprise you.

Most people who take the AMP discover that they "need" much more time than the 672 hours God has actually given us in any four-week period! Typically, we discover that our expectations for ourselves are out of line with the time God has made available. That, of course, means that our sense of what we ought to do is different from God's sense of that same thing. From one perspective, you could say that the excess hours you "need" are a precise indicator of how much you are out of God's will for your life. Whatever "oughts" add up to more time than God has given represent a misreading of his will for us. Some of us say yes to everything, and before long we have commitments that no one could fulfill—not even Jesus Christ. That syndrome is usually rooted in a fear of displeasing others rather than the fear of the Lord. But it illustrates the very practical way our time use intersects intensely spiritual and moral issues.

Marriage

In 1 Corinthians 7, Paul's discussion of marriage sheds light on the process of applying God's will to specific situations. In verse 39 he says, in regard to widows remarrying, "If her husband dies, she is free to marry anyone she wishes, but he must belong to the Lord." Notice that there is a clear prohibition of Christians marrying non-Christians. So within the circle of moral absolutes, Paul is very clear in forbidding a Christian to enter into such a relationship. Yet notice that he also says that she is free to marry whomever she wishes. Paul is not saying that a widow should not seek God's guidance about whom to marry, but that from the perspective of moral absolutes and prohibitions, she is free to marry as long as she marries a Christian.

Yet side by side with this freedom are guidelines and principles throughout this entire chapter that help determine whether a person should marry or stay single, including sexual self-control (v. 8), current conditions (vv. 29–31), and the burdens of marriage (vv. 32–35). Notice all the times in the chapter when Paul says, "I give you my advice." In such a decision we are clearly out of the realm of prohibitions and into the area of applied Christianity (circle two)—and therefore the area of guidance.

The choice of a mate should be a matter of prayer for guidance. The qualities of a godly woman or man are taught in numerous places in Scripture (Prov. 31:10–31; 1 Peter 3:1–7; Eph. 5:22–33; 1 Tim. 3:1–12) and require insight and wisdom from God—not only to discern their character, but to discern our own measure of faith, and our calling to care for and serve that specific person. Just because someone is a godly person does not mean you should marry him or her. A personal sense of calling to that ministry must be present, in much the same way we are called to minister our gifts in the church.

Food, Drink, and Honoraria

Food, drink, and payment for services provide another supposedly "less spiritual" area where the will of God is important to discern. You may be familiar with Paul's pivotal discussions regarding the use of Christian freedom in Romans 14 and 1 Corinthians 8–9. In both passages, Paul works out the implications of the love command so that we can see its application to very ordinary situations.

Regarding food and drink, Paul lays down the principle that we should not eat or drink in a way that will tempt a weaker brother to violate his own conscience. Paul affirms that eating meat offered to idols, even when it was served in the pagan temples, was not intrinsically sin. He is absolute about avoiding involvement in pagan worship (1 Cor. 10:17–22), yet he properly acknowledges that meat in itself is a blessing of God to be received with thanksgiving. With this balance in mind, if a brother's heart convicts him about it, we should not pressure him to eat meat left over from pagan sacrifice. For example, if you had a dinner guest and served him such meat, he would feel enormous pressure to eat it because he was your guest.

In our culture, alcoholic beverages, R-rated (and even PG-rated) videos, gambling, lotteries, tobacco products, rock music, and certain Lord's Day activities can all become occasions of stumbling for a brother or sister who is not certain such things are right before God. In such situations, Paul urges Christians whose hearts do not condemn them to abstain and not to use the freedom they might otherwise feel. Notice that Paul is not advocating abstinence from anything any other Christian may believe is wrong. He is advocating abstaining when your participation would tempt another Christian to participate against his conscience.

Paul even goes so far in 1 Corinthians 9 as to refuse payment for his ministry (and by implication the comfort of traveling with a Christian wife, see 1 Corinthians 9:5) in order not to burden the Corinthians or fuel the criticisms of Christ's enemies. Again we are faced with a decision about something that may be intrinsically good (receiving payment) but not God's moral preference for the individual in that situation. Paul made that decision because of his love for progress of the gospel and his desire to let nothing hinder its spread.

In verses 19–23, Paul states the guiding values that control his decisions in such cases. He says, "Though I am free and belong to no man, I make myself a slave to everyone, to win as many as possible" (v. 19). He adapts his personal lifestyle to be sometimes like a Jew, sometimes like a Gentile, sometimes like someone who is weak. "I have become all things to all men, so that by all possible means I may save some" (1 Cor. 9:22).

In this case, Paul is not just abstaining from things because of the weak, but adapting his entire lifestyle to eliminate barriers and promote unity with those with whom he worked. Paul doubtless had a strong personality and had numerous personal preferences in food, drink, observances, clothes, and relaxation, but they took a back seat to the nature of God's kingdom. "For the kingdom of God is not a matter of eating and drinking, but of righteousness, peace and joy in the Holy Spirit, because anyone who serves Christ in this way is pleasing to God" (Rom. 14:17–18). Paul was demonstrating the "good, pleasing and perfect will of God" (Rom. 12:2) he had described two chapters before.

There are other ways in which this principle is applied in Paul's writings: slaves contemplating seeking their freedom (1 Cor. 7:21), Christians tempted to become slaves for economic reasons (1 Cor. 7:23), unmarried Christians considering marriage (1 Cor. 7:8), widows considering remarriage (1 Cor. 7:39), and engaged couples who now doubt whether they ought to marry anyone (1 Cor. 7:25–38).[3]

I hope that this survey has demonstrated by principle and example that the will of God can be rooted in a positive command (love one another) yet apply to very specific (seemingly unspiritual) situations. It is exciting to think that God wants to work such wisdom in all of us—that the renewed mind can be ours in Jesus Christ.

Conclusion

God's will (that is, God's moral will—his commands and desires) is complex because of our personal and situational diversity. But it is also simple in the way it reflects the basic rule Christ laid down as the

---

3 This difficult passage is subject to a number of interpretations, but whatever the understanding, it represents an application of principles of God's kingdom to very specific situations.

essence of all that the Father revealed to him. Jesus completes that powerful passage in John 15:15–17 by simply saying, "Love one another." It is rather shocking that, after telling the disciples that he will reveal everything that he has learned from the Father, he would summarize it all by simply saying, "Love one another." He has described the greatest love as one that lays down its life for a friend (John 15:13). Jesus prepares them to love as they have been loved. That is the most profound guidance human beings will ever receive. And all of life is the outworking of that command.

Admittedly, most of us are a little disappointed at the generality of the advice. We would prefer Christ to reveal where we should go to college or whom to marry, or whether to take that tempting job offer. But while we shall see in the next chapter that God desires to guide us on these issues, he guides us by helping us make the connection to Christ, his purpose, and kingdom. If we do not understand the relevance of that connection to our situation, we have not really understood our situation. We are probably not ready for any other kind of "guidance." God equips us to be a people with a growing ability to make the connections between the everyday issues and the living God.

For Review and Reflection

1. What distinctions do some make between the "individual will of God" on the one hand, and the "moral will of God" and the "sovereign will of God" on the other hand?

2. After reading this chapter, do you think this is a biblical distinction?

3. What are the four problems with accepting the "bull's eye" view of the will of God?

4. Have you ever been caught in one of those problems? Describe it. How did you get out of it?

5. Have you sought guidance from God in the areas of money, use of gifts at church and on the job, time commitments, marriage, and lifestyle? Describe how you pursued this guidance and the outcome.

6. Have you had the experience of being given wisdom or insight into a situation and therefore being able to connect your decisions to the values and purposes of God? Describe what happened.

CHAPTER 7

GUIDANCE AND
CHRISTIAN LIBERTY

WE are now ready to look at the third concentric circle in our diagram of the will of God (see Figure 2).

This third, outside ring covers choices controlled by what theologians call "Christian liberty." This area of decision making marks out the territory where the Christian has freedom before God to make decisions based on personal preference.

The doctrine of Christian liberty comes from classic Reformation theology (Westminster Confession of Faith, 20). It refers to areas of life in which God leaves the believer's conscience free from the control of human standards and traditions that go beyond Scripture. It pertains to what are matters of human preference only, for which, therefore, no one can condemn another before God.

A classic example is the Christian's use of alcoholic beverages. Some churches began teaching (as far back as the Reformation) that any use of alcohol was sin. This became the predominant view in the American church during the temperance movement, when alcoholic beverages were banned by constitutional amendment. These leaders

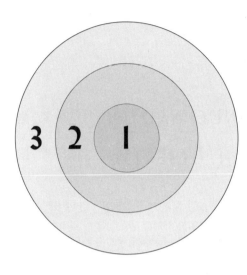

1. AREA OF THINGS PROHIBITED
   • "Put offs"
   • Requires obedience in all situations
   • Area of church discipline

2. AREA OF THE APPLICATION OF GOD'S POSITIVE COMMANDS
   • Guidance by wisdom and discernment
   • Can be in or out of God's will depending on the situation, motive, outcome, etc.

3. AREA OF CHRISTIAN LIBERTY
   • Choices between equally good alternatives
   • Providential guidance (small "g")
   • Motive must be to glorify God

Figure 2. The three circles of God's will

argued that since alcohol was the cause of so much evil, Christians must be required to abstain.

Other church leaders maintained the traditional position, that this was a matter of Christian liberty. They taught that so long as alcohol was not misused by drunkenness, no church had the right to add such a human law to the requirement of God's Word. These churches pointed out the stern warnings that Jesus issued to the Pharisees of his day, condemning them because they taught the commandments of men as if they were the laws of God (Matt. 15:3–11).

Other issues were also debated under the heading of Christian liberty: social dancing, smoking, rock music, jazz, movies, war, and holding political office. Churches decided that either none, some, or all of these were sins and therefore forbidden to Christians.

In the New Testament, this issue of defining the limits of Christian freedom was one of the most volatile. Converted Jews brought the Old Testament dietary and ritual traditions with them into the churches. Gentile converts did not know to what extent they were required to keep these Old Testament laws. In addition, certain practices of the Gentiles generated extreme controversy.

In Romans 14, Paul deals with the controversy regarding whether Christians should eat meat or be vegetarians. Because it is an example of applied love (living out the positive commands of Scripture), we dealt with it briefly in the previous chapter. Now let's look at it from the perspective of Christian liberty.

Paul made it clear that this was an issue of Christian liberty (Rom. 14:14) and therefore personal choice, with three exceptions. First, if you believe it is wrong to eat meat, you should abstain until you are convinced otherwise. Second, if you are eating with a conscientious vegetarian, you should not serve him (or yourself) meat because that would pressure him to violate his own conscience. It would be wrong for the vegetarian because he thinks it is, or might be, wrong (Rom. 14:23). The third exception is this: We are not to look down upon or condemn those who could not eat meat (or practice other things that fell into the same category).

In 1 Corinthians 10:14–33, Paul deals with yet another issue of Christian liberty, the issue of eating meat previously offered to idols. Some Christians ate such meat and others objected strenuously. Again Paul confirms that meat is created by God and is fine to eat if one can eat it with thanksgiving and a clean conscience. However, the apostle gives the same warning to the Corinthians that he gave to the Romans. Those who eat such meat should not use their liberty to hurt or destroy "weaker" brothers whose consciences would condemn them if they ate. Paul again illustrates it with the social situation of a meal. He tells the "strong" not to tempt the "weak" by serving meat offered to idols or by demeaning his commitment.

Below are some of the situational factors that determine whether something is in the area of Christian liberty (our third circle) or the moral area of applied love (our second circle).

If a decision falls into this third circle of Christian liberty, God has no preference (will) in the situation. He holds us responsible to make our own decisions. This is the area where God has given us great freedom to order our lives according to our own preferences.

How do we know what falls into this area? Simply put, by a process of elimination. First, ask if the decision is prohibited by Scripture (circle one). If it is not, then ask whether the decision is controlled by the applied wisdom of Scripture (circle two). If it is not, then we know that it belongs to the large range of decisions where all the alternatives are good, just, and right in God's sight (circle three). Some theologians have called them "things indifferent" to moral decision making. But since these are options that have passed muster in circles one and two, they are properly called "things lawful and good." If the issue does not belong in circle one or circle two, then it is a matter of Christian liberty.

Let me illustrate. If you are considering an activity prohibited directly by Scripture (adultery) or by deduction from Scripture (abortion), it is wrong to engage in it (circle one). If the activity is not prohibited in Scripture but is wrong from the perspective of applied love—the application of the positive commandments (circle two)—then it, too, is not an area of Christian liberty. Paul's illustrations urge us not to use liberty to wound a weaker believer. For example, going to the shore for a weekend fishing trip might be a matter of Christian liberty for most people, but if my responsibilities with my wife or child are compromised, my decision is in circle two, not circle three.

Yet we make hundreds of decisions each day where God calls us to exercise our freedom (circle three). I do not have to seek to know God's will (normally) on which pair of dark socks I will wear today or whether or not to wear a jacket. Garry Friesen's point is well taken here—it is wrong to envision God as even having a "personal will" for us in this area.

In fact, it is better to think of believers as sons and daughters of the King—with authority to live, to decide, and to choose freely in the vast area of the circumstances of their lives.

That is a precious freedom and liberty that Christ purchased on the cross for believers, and Paul especially reminds the Galatian Christians that it must be guarded. In the Old Testament, God gave many burdensome laws pertaining to every aspect of life: diet, calendar, cleanliness, marriage, engagement, dispute resolution, worship, economy, criminal and civil law, and many more. These sanctions and rules were necessary because the Messiah's work was not completed and the Spirit of God had not come. Jesus says that the divorce laws were given because of the "hardness of heart" of Israel (Matt. 19:8). With the giving of the Spirit, the veil has been taken away from the eyes of the Gentiles and the full glory of God's image can be seen, known, and obeyed without the external restraints of civil penalty, ritual, sacrifice, and discipline.

Yet many of Jewish descent in the New Testament church were eager to retain all the Old Testament ordinances, along with the traditions that had built up around them. Paul strongly forbids the Galatians from going back to the old, weak, and burdensome ways. Paul exclaims, "It is for freedom that Christ has set us free. Stand firm, then, and do not let yourselves be burdened again by a yoke of slavery" (Gal. 5:1). So we can see that there are profound issues at stake in defending this third circle of Christian liberty. God has delegated large areas of personal responsibility and decision making to us and left us free, in this area, to "love him and do as we please."

While God's sovereign plan covers every detail of our lives, by contrast, his will and preferences for our lives leave large areas where personal preference and decision rule. God may not care whether I buy a Chevy or Ford pickup, whether I subscribe to CompuServe or America Online, or whether I go fishing in saltwater or freshwater. If two colleges are identical in what they offer my son, I will not blame him if he goes to one by the ocean with great skiing nearby in winter.

To recap then, Christians are free forever from a fear-driven need to make sure that every choice they make is "according to God's will." That attitude in itself is out of God's will! Part of the wisdom we seek is the insight to tell the difference between choices that are equally good and choices that only appear that way!

In fact, in our example of Rick, a friend had told him that he was so good at graphic design that it did not matter whether he stayed an employee or opened his own business. He would be successful either way. The friend was saying that it was only a matter of personal preference and had nothing to do with God's wisdom. It turned out that the friend was wrong. Rick's decision was in the second circle, not the third. It was not a matter of choosing between equally good alternatives because Rick was not using his full capabilities as an employee, and God had gifted him with abilities and faith to run his own business.

To say that a decision falls within the third circle is not to say that it is insignificant. When General Douglas MacArthur led the invasion of the Korean Peninsula during the Korean War, he knew that the outcome of the war depended on his success. He also knew that without the element of surprise, the invasion could easily be a disaster costing thousands of lives needlessly. He could not obtain any reliable information on whether the communist forces knew of his invasion plans. He had to guess, and he ordered the invasion based on his guess. The invasion was a success because the communist forces were completely surprised.

The decision to deploy troops in a particular tactical way is largely a matter of human choice, yet often the consequences are huge. No amount of biblical meditation will give a commander direction for battlefield tactics. The choice of battlefield tactics, as a decision, is not usually a decision rooted in biblical principles.

The choice about entering the war in the first place certainly is. The overall military strategy may be affected by biblical ethics, and his motivation certainly must be. But after having scanned the situation for those factors, whether or not to attack without intelligence reports is not something that can normally be decided by appeal to the commandments of God or the applied wisdom of God. Nor do I believe God had an individual will that MacArthur should have sought to know for the tactical decision.

Having said this, however, anyone with so much at stake would be foolish not to pray and ask for faithfulness in his duties and for the courage to make the necessary decisions. Additionally, he should pray for God's providential blessing on the gathering of intelligence and his help with the invasion decision itself. From a biblical perspective, though, he is not praying for guidance but for *success*. God might well bless him with ideas, facts that come to light, clear hunches, etc., but that is not guidance to know the will of God. It is God's providential ordering of circumstances to help a burdened man.

Let me give a more personal illustration. I can drive to work any one of three ways. Each route has its advantages and disadvantages. I normally choose a route based entirely on my mood, which is usually controlled by the time of day. The route I take is largely a matter of personal choice, yet by taking one particular route rather than another I may avoid a life-threatening car accident, or I may be involved in one. Again, there *are* providential consequences to decisions made within the realm of Christian liberty, but God does not expect or desire us to discern or guess his providential will in such situations. He allows and insists that we make the decisions.

Once we are in the realm of Christian liberty—that is, within the range of equally valid options—the guardrail of providence is the only way that God helps (guides) us. We might call it guidance with a small "g." God in his providence can put thoughts into our heads, but that is not true guidance. It is the operation of God's providence. The thought may enter my head, "Don't take the normal route home today." I cannot tell whether the source of the thought is God, Satan, or the salami sandwich I had for lunch, but I am free to respond to it if I wish. Many of our decisions are made on hunches. Sometimes they are right and sometime horribly wrong—especially when I am lost and looking for a church where I am supposed to be speaking in ten minutes.

Sometimes God provides unusual and extraordinary providences that greatly assist us. These can come in answer to prayer. They can be in the form of the provision of food, money, or safety, and they can come in the form of ideas or thoughts. Many discoveries in science have been made in answer to the prayers of Christians.

That God answers prayer for such help was impressed on me in an unusual way by my grandfather, Dr. Harry Johnston. In response to his prayer for God's help in finding a chemical compound, he developed root canal therapy (endodontia) to save abscessed teeth from extraction. In the 1940s he wrote about the experience as follows:

> I was particularly distressed at finding it necessary to extract anteriors for girls and women and [then] try to secure efficient and cosmetic effects with bridgework. I found that the loss of one or more of these more prominent teeth had a very disastrous psychological effect on many of the young girls and women, making them in many cases very self-conscious and shy, and in some cases apparently completely spoiling the joyous, carefree, happy disposition of the patient.

I made inquiries and studied all the methods and materials from the journals and books on such subjects, looking for some improvement in the method of treating these teeth, but was not able to make any substantial improvement in the results. I was fully convinced that there was a way in which infection could be controlled in the apical areas as well as it was in other areas of the body, and I became so obsessed with this idea that I entered into a series of experiments and research— working almost night and day for three years. . . . After three years, I had completely exhausted all ideas as to further research and found myself at the end of a blind alley.

Having been reared in a Christian family and gone through the delightful experience of "conversion" some years before, I was convinced that there was no evil of any sort in the world that God did not have a remedy for. After thinking this over for some time, I decided to submit myself and my problem to Him. So, that night on my knees beside my bed, I expressed my desire to the Lord, stating that I knew if there was a remedy in existence for this, He knew and would reveal it to me, or if there was not one, He could easily provide one and reveal it to me. I pledged myself that if He would do this, I would give Him all the glory and the credit; would not try to reap great personal profit from it; would give it freely to the profession and teach it to any other dentist without cost to him. I prayed about this daily for three months, getting no sign, no indication that God heard me or intended to do anything about it, but I was determined to persist until I came to some positive result. At about the end of the three months, I was by the chair one morning working on a rather difficult three-surface inlay preparation on a lower first molar, and while at pin-point concentration on this effort, suddenly there obtruded itself into my mind, pushing all other thoughts aside, one word which came just as clearly as if someone had spoken it to me from the door. In fact, I looked up to see if that were the case, but there was no one there. That word was IODINE, and with it came the realization that this was the answer to my prayer and problem. I was not easily convinced, however, that this could be the answer as I had extensively experimented with iodine and gotten no result.

After some initial problems, my grandfather located the right compound of iodine and within a week had successfully treated his first patient, saving a severely abscessed tooth for a twelve-year-old girl. I have included this lengthy account just because it illustrates so clearly the dynamic of God's providential provision of the information he needed in response to prayer. That provision did not stand on God's promise of providing guidance about his will. Rather, it was wonderful, providential help. But do not confuse dramatic stories like this with what God promises us in biblical guidance and the development of spiritual wisdom.

These "strange providences" can also come to us for no apparent reason, without prayer. For example, my grandmother (the wife of the dentist mentioned above) was eating Sunday dinner with her family when the phone rang. She spontaneously said, "Uncle Fred died." She then answered the phone and, sure enough, Uncle Fred, whom no one had heard from since he had moved to Japan the previous year, had suddenly died. Such premonitions, predictions, and hunches are under this category of God's providence. They do not constitute guidance in the true sense of the word. They should be treated in the same way as any information that God may bring across your path—such as a news report, a friend, or a book. You cannot tell whether it is correct, valid, or helpful apart from testing it—just as you would any other information.

Notice that God does not promise to provide these extraordinary thoughts or ideas to us in the same way he promises to provide wisdom to us. All who seek wisdom will find it (James 1:5), but God will not always provide the providential circumstances or ideas we may wish he would give us. He does promise, however, to work in all things for our transformation into Christ's image—even when he says no and does not answer a prayer for help or success.

In describing this third circle of Christian liberty, there are two important qualifications to make. First, at the motive level, nothing is "indifferent." Paul tells us in 1 Corinthians 10:31, "So whether you eat or drink or whatever you do, do it all for the glory of God." He also tells us that whatever we do, we must do it with all of our hearts as unto the Lord. So to be "theologically correct," we must speak of things in the outer circle as *relatively* indifferent.

In other words, in this area God has revealed no preference about our choices between this and that, but he is not indifferent to our *motives* about which one we choose. Let's say that one morning I choose to wear a brown shirt instead of a blue one. I can ask myself, *Am I dressing for God's glory or for my own? Am I dressing to gain attention or to serve others?* Our motives for everything we do are always deeply and spiritually relevant to our relationship to God. We do things for God's glory or for our own.

Second, the boundary between the positive commands (the second circle) and the "equally good alternatives" in the third circle blur into each other—at least from a human perspective. It is much like the way Earth's atmosphere gradually gives way to space as a rocket goes higher and higher. There is not a hard boundary but a progressive transition from circle two (positive, situational obedience) to circle three (equally good alternatives).

In Figure 2, the realm of morally equal options is so large that it could be appropriately represented by outer space. We never really get to the end of it. It represents the area where God's guidance is through

CHARACTERISTICS OF DECISION MAKING	CIRCLE 1 (INNER CIRCLE)	CIRCLE 2 (MIDDLE CIRCLE)	CIRCLE 3 (OUTER CIRCLE)
Direction Obtained By:	Knowledge of God's Law	Wisdom and Discernment	Personal Choice
Moral Status of the Decision Making	Moral Absolutes	Applied Love	Morally Equal Options (Pass Test of 1 and 2)
Decision Making Based On:	Prohibitions in Scripture	Positive Commands	Christian Liberty
God's Role in Decision Making	Revelation (Deut. 29:29)	Illumination (1 Cor. 2:1–15)	Providence
Role of Motives	Godly or Ungodly Motives (James 4:1–4)	Godly or Ungodly Motives (1 Cor. 13:1–2)	Godly or Ungodly Motives (2 Cor. 10:31)

Figure 3. Summary of the three circles of guidance

providence and ours is through personal human choice. This human choice is no threat to God's sovereign plan for our lives because no matter what complicated sets of choices we make, God's wisdom and power effortlessly weave them into his plan for our lives. Our liberty is only child's play compared to the power of God's management of the universe.

Summary Chart: The Three Circles of Guidance

Before we dive into crucial biblical texts promising wisdom as the means to guidance, we should review the grand landscape we have already traversed. Figure 3 shows the nature of the decision making that takes place in each of the three circles. It describes God's relationship to it, the role of situations, the role of motives, and its relationship to biblical truth. It summarizes in convenient form what we have covered so far.

For Review and Reflection

1. What is Christian liberty?

2. What kinds of issues fell into this category for Christians in biblical times? What issues are debated today?

3. Why is there so much more freedom for the Christian than there was for the Jew under Old Testament law?

4. How are Christians supposed to use that freedom?

5. From your own life, give an example of something that might be "indifferent" in itself (and therefore a matter of Christian liberty), but which circumstances make a matter of love toward another person. How did you handle it?

6. What is the distinction between God granting guidance and God granting help or success?

7. In what way is the area of Christian liberty still moral, and only relatively "indifferent"?

PART THREE *Experiencing Guidance*

CHAPTER 8

GUIDANCE AND THE
WISDOM OF GOD

SO far, we have covered a lot of territory on the divine guidance
issue. The central idea of this book is that discernment is the key to
knowing God's will for your life and for specific situations. We have argued that this area of decision making (circle two) is quite different
from obeying the prohibitions of Scripture (circle one) or exercising
personal choice of taste, expediency, mood, etc. (circle three) among
morally good alternatives.

We are now ready to examine the positive teaching of Scripture that
supports the central truth—that we come to know the will of God by
discernment, wisdom, and insight. The purpose of this book is to show
that the Bible's answer to our need for guidance boils down to one very
rich word: wisdom. From various perspectives, wisdom is also seen as
discernment, insight, discretion, prudence, and understanding, depending on the context.

The question remains, however, "Is this truth explicitly taught in
Scripture?" Does the Bible directly state that the way to know the will
of God is through spiritual wisdom, discernment, and insight? I believe the answer is yes.

The Knowledge of His Will

There are at least five key passages in the New Testament that teach us how to actually know God's will. None of these are narrative passages that describe past events (like the conversion of the apostle Paul). This is helpful, because although narrative passages are important for many reasons, they must be interpreted by other passages to determine their meaning. The passages we will look at are ones whose purpose is to teach us what to believe and do.

Colossians 1:9–10 is the first. Paul writes,

> *For this reason, since the day we heard about you, we have not stopped praying for you and asking God to fill you with the knowledge of his will through all spiritual wisdom and understanding. And we pray this in order that you may live a life worthy of the Lord and may please him in every way: bearing fruit in every good work, growing in the knowledge of God.*

According to Paul, knowledge of the will of God comes through "all spiritual wisdom and understanding." The phrase "will of God" does not refer to God's decretive will (the will of God's sovereign plan) because that belongs to God alone (Deut. 29:29). The phrase refers to God's will in the sense of what God wants, commands, and desires to happen. It is used the same way Jesus used it when he prayed, "Thy will be done, on earth as it is in heaven." This is God's preceptive will.

So Paul is praying that the Colossian church would have a knowledge of God's preceptive will. What Paul envisions is not that these believers would have a bare remembrance of the prohibitions of the Ten Commandments (Ex. 20:1–17). He wants their lives to be a rich reflection of all God's positive commands for an individual's life. The will of God includes commands to love our marriage partners; bring up our children; minister to the poor, the prisoner, the widow; support our family; share the gospel with others; put our heart into our vocation as unto Christ; use our gifts within the body of Christ; give generously of our money and time; and a myriad of other implications. It is the fulfilling of the whole law in loving God and loving our neighbor as we have been loved by God.

This kind of wisdom enables us to set priorities for a positive life in the midst of a culture that throws "obligations" at us a mile a minute. It is wisdom that enables us to establish our calling, exercise our gifts, and buy up our opportunities to embody the positive will of God. To be sure, obedience to the prohibitions of Scripture is also of absolute importance. We spend our lives putting to death the sin that takes us captive through temptation. Paul tells the Colossians to "rid [them]selves of all such things as these: anger, rage, malice, slander, and filthy language from your lips" (Col. 3:8). But there is an equal emphasis on putting on the new life in Christ. In Colossians 3:12 he says,

> Therefore, as God's chosen people, holy and dearly loved, clothe yourselves with compassion, kindness, humility, gentleness and patience. . . . Teach and admonish one another with all wisdom. . . . Wives, submit to your husbands. . . . Husbands, love your wives. . . . Children, obey your parents. . . . Slaves, obey your earthly masters. . . . Masters, . . . provide what is right and fair. . . . Devote yourselves to prayer, being watchful and thankful. (Col. 3:12–4:2)

God's positive commandments are open-ended; just as open-ended as the love of God that motivates us to keep them. In that sense, love fulfills law. For this reason there will never be any system for discerning the will of God that reduces obedience to a set of behaviors and procedures for every situation. Remember the parable of the Good Samaritan. The priest and Levite crossed over onto the other side of the road to avoid encountering the wounded victim (Luke 10:25–37). They believed that as long as they did not commit a prohibited act, their duty was done. Jesus pointed out that the will of God was to positively love our neighbor as the Samaritan traveler did the victim.

We sinners do not like open-ended commands. We can't be in control with them, especially when the commands are hard to fulfill because of our sin. There is no way to cross off "Love your neighbor as yourself" from your "To Do" list at the end of the day!

Paul, however, is praying for the Colossians to know the will of God "in order that you may live a life worthy of the Lord and may please him in every way: bearing fruit in every good work" (Col. 1:10). Paul had a very high outcome in mind when he prayed for them to know the will of God. His description of that outcome is what any Christian should long to have said about his life. What higher outcome could be contemplated for this earth? What a glorious destiny awaits those who seek to know the will of God! This is a goal we will never fully attain in this life. We are called to ask God continually to fill us with a deeper knowledge of himself and his will. To summarize then, we can safely say that guidance is knowledge of the will of God, which comes by wisdom and understanding.

Approving the Will of God

It is interesting to note that Paul begins his letter to the Philippians striking the same theme. This is the second passage we will consider. He says in Philippians 1:9–11,

> And this is my prayer: that your love may abound more and more in knowledge and depth of insight, so that you may be able to discern what is best and may be pure and blameless until the day of Christ, filled with the fruit of righteousness that comes through Jesus Christ—to the glory and praise of God.

Here, instead of discerning the will of God, Paul says "discerning what is best" or, as the King James Version says, "that you may approve the things that are excellent." The underlying Greek word is the word for testing, trying, or proving.

It closely parallels Paul's teaching in Romans 12:1–2, which is the third passage we will visit:

> *Therefore, I urge you, brothers, in view of God's mercy, to offer your bodies as living sacrifices, holy and pleasing to God—this is your spiritual act of worship. Do not conform any longer to the pattern of this world, but be transformed by the renewing of your mind. Then you will be able to test and approve what God's will is—his good, pleasing and perfect will.*

Paul says that a renewed mind will result in the ability to "approve" or "show" what is the will of God—the good, the well-pleasing, and the perfect. It is the same Greek word used in Philippians 1:9.

This word "approve" is well chosen to describe the process of "discovering, finding out and learning by experience just how good, well-pleasing and perfect the will of God is" (Murray 1965, 115). John Murray, in his comments on Romans 12:1–2, writes,

> If life is aimless, stagnant, fruitless, lacking in content, it is because we are not entering by experience into the richness of God's will. The commandment of God is exceeding broad. There is not a moment of life that the will of God does not command, no circumstance that it does not fill with meaning if we are responsive to the fullness of his revealed counsel for us. (Murray 1965, 115)

It is like the story my pastor recently related of a honeymoon couple who reserved the best room in the airport hotel for their first night together. They were to fly out the next morning. They arrived late and were exhausted. They opened the door to their room with great anticipation and saw only a small room with a rather small bed. They checked their room number: it was correct. They called the front desk and said how dissatisfied they were. But there were no other rooms available. They decided just to rough it for the one night rather than raise an upsetting furor.

The next morning at breakfast they saw a picture in the lobby advertising their room and noticed a familiar-looking door. They realized that the door they thought led to the room next door was the door that led into the main part of their room. They rushed back upstairs, flung open the door in question and were greeted by the sight of a huge, gorgeous room, with all the amenities they had missed the night before. They were in the right room, but they had not opened the door to the main part of it. It turned out to be a two-room suite and they had stayed in the auxiliary room.

It can be the same way for us if we focus only on the prohibitions of God's will and not the positive commands. We can miss experiencing the good, pleasing, and perfect will of God if we are not progressively transformed by the renewing of our minds.

There is a fourth passage where Paul explains that the way to know God's will for one's life or situation is through wisdom, discernment, and insight. Ephesians 5:15–17 specifically considers the use of time and God's will. There Paul focuses on establishing priorities. He states,

> *Be very careful, then, how you live—not as unwise but as wise, making the most of every opportunity, because the days are evil. Therefore do not be foolish, but understand what the Lord's will is. Do not get drunk on wine. . . . Instead, be filled with the Spirit.*

In this remarkable passage, Paul is applying his own teaching. He tells believers not to live the unexamined life, but rather to give great care as to how they live. He identifies wisdom as the key to knowing how to make the most of the time and opportunities that remain. Time must be wrested away from the control of evil ("redeemed" in the KJV) for God's use. If we only react passively, we will miss the positive opportunities God has afforded us to do his will. He warns of foolishness, which in this context is the great enemy of knowing the will of God. Paul then refers to the need to bring all of life under the controlling influence (the filling) of the Spirit of God, rather than under the controlling influence of alcohol or any other life-dominating force. He spends the next thirty verses (Eph. 5:20–6:20) describing this Spirit-filled life and the core priorities in seven positive areas of God's commandments.

Paul never suggests that God's people should seek God's will through circumstances, hunches, a sense of "leading" or other means. There can be little doubt that if you or I asked Paul how to know the will of God, he would say, "Seek wisdom and insight so that you can understand how the message of the Bible applies to your life." He would tell husbands to love their wives, wives to respect their husbands, children to honor their parents, workers to obey their masters, working from the heart as unto Christ, and masters to give their workers what is right and fair. Above all, he would tell us to build ourselves up spiritually so as to be victorious under Satan's attack. Becoming sensitive to the core priorities in each area and assimilating them into our lives enables us to know and do the will of God.

The Search for Wisdom

The last passage we will consider is in the book of James. James is the only book in the New Testament patterned after the wisdom literature of the Old Testament. It is a kind of New Testament book of Proverbs. It is not surprising that James, like Proverbs, begins immediately with the question of how to obtain wisdom. James, the brother of Jesus, writes in 1:5–7,

> *If any of you lacks wisdom, he should ask God, who gives generously to all without finding fault, and it will be given to him. But when he asks, he must believe and not doubt, because he who doubts is like a wave of the sea, blown and tossed by the wind. That man should not think he will receive anything from the Lord; he is a double-minded man, unstable in all he does.*

James is discussing "trials of many kinds." He promises that those who allow God to disciple them through trials will develop perseverance that will result in maturity, making us complete and lacking nothing. Perhaps writing the word "lacking" triggered James's next thought, "If any of you lack wisdom. . . ." Among Christians there is almost a universal sense of a lack of wisdom. It is also possible that James moves to the issue of wisdom specifically because one of the most difficult aspects of any trial is not knowing what to do.

The promise of James 1:5–7 states that "any of you" who lacks wisdom can ask God. He will grant it if we do not doubt our request. Wisdom is the ability to apply the will of God. It makes the connection between the commandment and the situation. Wisdom makes Christians different in the real world, and enables us to understand how God's own values apply to a situation (James 3:17–18). Wisdom knows how to love one's enemies as Christ loved us. It discerns the path of peace between those in conflict (1 Cor. 6:1–8; James 3:18). In fact, James 1:5 ties us directly to the book of Proverbs, which is largely dedicated to the description of wisdom, how it is obtained, and its outcome.

In Proverbs 2:1–4 we read,

My son, if you accept my words
  and store up my commands within you,
turning your ear to wisdom
  and applying your heart to understanding,
and if you call out for insight
  and cry aloud for understanding,
and if you look for it as silver
  and search for it as for hidden treasure,
then you will understand the fear of the LORD
  and find the knowledge of God.

Notice the similarity to Colossians 1:9–11, where the one who uses wisdom gains more wisdom and knowledge of God.

Solomon also says,

Blessed is the man who finds wisdom,
  the man who gains understanding,
for she is more profitable than silver
  and yields better returns than gold.
She is more precious than rubies;
  nothing you desire can compare with her.
    (Prov. 3:13–15)

It is clear that the desire for wisdom is a basic mark of righteousness and should burn within the heart of every child of God.

Solomon lived out this priority in his early life. God appeared to Solomon in Gibeon after he had offered a thousand offerings on the altar. (He must have had a lot of sin to confess!) God spoke to him in a dream and told him he could have anything he requested from

God. God did not invite Solomon to ask for wisdom (as James is doing). He just gave him a "blank check." Solomon responded, "So give your servant a discerning heart to govern your people and to distinguish between right and wrong" (1 Kings 3:9).

Solomon knew the law of God; it was the challenge of applying it that made it clear that he was "but a child" (1 Kings 3:7). God blessed Solomon and gave him the wisdom he desired, as well as power and riches he did not specifically ask for.

When someone judges cases as Solomon had to do, he must know more than the precepts of God. He must be able to apply them to the cases and situations in life. That challenge will drive us to our knees to seek the same wisdom Solomon sought. Without it, we will continue to spout the wonderful truths of God but we will not be living them. We will not walk worthy of the Lord and will not bear fruit in every good work. We will dishonor the Lord by confessing what we do not live out in the nitty-gritty of life.

What is wisdom? How is it defined biblically? The word can be used in different ways, but I believe that wisdom is the moral skill to understand and apply the commandments of God to situations and people. It is the ability to connect the principle to the application. It particularizes and personalizes the will, priorities, and preferences of God. This is the quality James pleads for among Christians, who are to be doers of the Word of God and not hearers only.

In a similar vein, Robert Hicks adapts the definition of Allen Ross and defines wisdom as moral skill and mental discernment (Hicks 1995, 16). As Hicks put it,

> Proverbs is trying to make us all a little street smart. . . . To live righteously from the perspective of the wisdom literature is not to be a monk, isolated in a cave. It is to be where the action is,

in the mess and stench of life, engaging and enhancing the lives of others. (p. 19)

Hicks rightly notes that Lady Wisdom (Prov. 1:20–21) posts herself not in the university lecture hall but on the street, in the gates, in the square, in the city. "She stations herself at these life intersections and cries, 'Come to me and learn wisdom' " (p. 21).

Wisdom is not intelligence or a vast store of factual information. It is not cleverness at obtaining one's goals. It is the ability to apply in life the character and purposes of God. The wise individual discerns and lives out the unseen reality of God's kingdom and rule. In that sense, attaining it is the highest goal in life (Prov. 3:13–15; 4:7–9).

I fear that we have lost this focus in discussions about knowing the will of God. In our churches, Christian schools, and colleges, the desire for wisdom is not talked about, not promoted, not even offered very often—except as a short-term fix to a bad problem. The emphasis is more on the development of intelligence, the prerequisite to a successful college experience, which leads to a successful career. We hear, "God gave you a brain—use it!"

I meet very few Christians who say that they are seeking wisdom from God as the means to knowing and doing his will. It often appears that wealth, recognition, and success are more prominent, and wisdom is reduced to cleverness in attaining these and similar desires. Yet the promise of James 1:5–7 should strongly motivate us to seek wisdom, with the full expectation that God himself will keep his word. This is not a request he will turn down.

Why We Might Not Want Wisdom

Yet there is an important condition attached to the promise. The seeker for wisdom must want the wisdom that comes from God "without doubting." This refers first of all to doubt as to whether God *can* provide wisdom to a sinner perplexed by trials. I believe it also refers to doubt as to whether the seeker really *wants* God's wisdom with all his heart. Will the seeker give up when the going gets tough? Will she fall away when the search for wisdom does not produce the particular temporal blessings she has hoped for?

The reference to the "double-minded" man highlights this second implication. "Double-minded" is the translation of a Greek word that literally means "double-souled." Such a person is not sure if he really wants to follow the wisdom from God. He is not wholeheartedly consecrated to having his life be the expression of God's will. For a while, he may try living this way to "see if it works." But, when his goals are not realized, he quickly reverts to wisdom from below (James 3:13–15). He seeks to find a clever means to get his way and still look good. He goes back and forth like a wave driven by the wind. In James 4:8, the double-minded are told to "purify your hearts." It is a heart problem, not an intellectual problem. James gives the same strong moral condemnation here as he does to the impure motives that cause "quarrels and fights among you" (James 4:1).

James 3:13–18 gives us some idea of why people might think they want the wisdom from God, but then change their minds as they start to learn it. Wisdom requires learning to accomplish deeds in humility, yet most of us want wisdom partly because it adds to our stature. James says that wisdom is peace-loving, and that sounds wonderful until we find out we will not be able to expose or condemn someone who has sinned against us. The wisdom from above is considerate. That also sounds appealing until we realize that we may have to think of someone else's needs for a lifetime and serve him or her with little or no earthly thanks. Submission is not something that most of us love to learn. It grates against our preference to be in control.

We like to think of ourselves as full of mercy until we realize that we may have to spend years being merciful to a family member who does not deserve it, and who, on top of that, spreads false and derogatory information about us. Being a peacemaker might seem fulfilling because we visualize God bringing the other party around to a "reasonable" position, but then we find out that peace will often have to be unilaterally imposed. It will require us to overlook an offense and endure being wronged (1 Cor. 6:1–8). This is the life of the Sermon on the Mount. It is the life of love for our enemies, even when they are the members of our own household, company, or family. When love of our enemies is required, lots of people decide to abandon the search for godly wisdom. They opt for a kind of wisdom that seeks ways of getting their desires fulfilled, all the while appearing to be benevolent, peaceful, and generous.

But for those who stay the course, for those who accept the growth and insight God gives them through trials, for those who do not give up seeking to express the law of God in all of life, for those who make it their life goal to express the life of Christ—they will grow to become wise. As Solomon said in Proverbs 3:18, "She is a tree of life to those who embrace her; those who lay hold on her will be blessed."

I think of a young woman who, after living with her boyfriend for three years, became a Christian ten days before their wedding day. In a heart-rending decision she broke up with him because he had no interest in Christ. She traveled the Christian singles road for six years without one serious date. Her old boyfriend was not one to give up and vigorously pursued her during those years. Though struggling with discouragement and some depression, she continued to serve Christ and the church with hospitality, secretarial help, mercy, and personal encouragement. She continued to love God and show love to others in her unique ways, instead of nursing disappointment in Christian men or in God himself. God used this to develop a wonderful character in her, which reflected itself in a growing, godly beauty (1 Peter 3:1–3). God did finally bless her with a fine Christian husband and family—in which she shines as someone who bears fruit in every good work.

We have looked at how Paul prayed for the Ephesian, Colossian, and Philippian Christians to be given wisdom. Now James invites us to do the same. Both James and Paul see the quest for wisdom as an ongoing effort throughout the believer's life. Bruce Waltke comments on this point when he says,

> Wisdom in the Old Testament is a character trait, not simply thinking soberly. People with wisdom have the character to make good decisions. (Waltke 1995, 36)

That makes the desire for wisdom a lifelong quest. Paul prayed for the Colossians and Philippians to be filled with wisdom every time he remembered them. So in James we have a description of a lifetime prayer request, not just a prayer in a moment of panic when our well-laid plans go awry. Rather, James says, "If any man lacks wisdom, he should ask God" (to make him wise).

We also see the quest for wisdom expressed in the actions of the twelve-year-old Jesus. He went to the temple and asked questions of the elders. He was hungry to know the Scriptures and posed questions to learn how they fit together. It is no wonder that Jesus was described as "filled with wisdom," having "the grace of God . . . upon him" (Luke 2:40).

Jesus intentionally based his decisions on the wisdom of God. Before Christ chose his twelve disciples, Luke records that he "went out to a mountainside to pray, and spent the night praying to God. When morning came, he called his disciples to him and chose twelve" (Luke 6:12–13). Christ had already spent considerable time with his closest followers. He knew them well. Yet he still sought wisdom and direction from God. Here the divine Son of God spends all night in prayer before making the choice of the Twelve. If Jesus had to pray, how much more should we seek God for wisdom in significant decisions? Jesus had no internal sin to cloud his mind, yet he also needed wisdom for discernment into the character of the twelve apostles he was about to choose.

We are now in a position to summarize the overall meaning of this teaching. Rather than being treated as servants, subject to a stream of directives, we are offered the very mind and wisdom of Christ. We are his friends. With the Word of God and the Spirit, we grow to see our environment with the eyes of Christ. We have the mind of Christ. Guidance is not a series of miscellaneous directives from God; it is God-wrought illumination of our understanding.

Knofel Staton defines it beautifully.

> Having wisdom is having God's disposition or characteristics within us as motivation and guidance in our decision making. (Staton 1968, 40)

Wisdom: The Truly Supernatural Gift

From a biblical perspective, wisdom is more miraculous and supernatural than any prophecy or directly inspired revelation. In this marvelous work, God progressively transforms sinners to think like himself, with God's priorities, sensitivities, agenda, and love. That is the greatest miracle ever accomplished by our Lord, though it may not be valued as such by a church hungry for more tangible signs and wonders.

This biblical and "miraculous" method of finding guidance is not well promoted in evangelical circles. The publishing houses turn out books by the dozen on guidance, but few emphasize wisdom. Unfortunately, most suggest and then attempt to regulate more questionable but supposedly "supernatural" methods.

James Ryle in his interesting book *Dream Come True* finds himself in exactly that dilemma. He strongly encourages believers to interpret their dreams by looking for the voice and direction of God, and he gives eight steps to prepare oneself for God to speak in a dream (Ryle 1995, 197). Yet the last of the eight steps is "Apply Your Heart to Wisdom." In this last step he says that everything we receive in a dream should be put through the screen of wisdom. In fact, he has a wonderful plea for believers to seek and value wisdom.

I very much agree with Ryle's desire to keep Christians from doing bizarre things based on dreams, and I certainly agree with the need to subject everything to biblical wisdom. The problem is that Ryle is being very inconsistent in telling people, on the one hand, to look to dreams for direct communication from God and then telling them, on the other hand, to subject it to their flawed and finite judgment. If Ryle expects God to speak directly to us, not mediated through the Bible, then we need to subordinate whatever human wisdom we have to that fresh revelation from God contained in the dream. If, however, God speaks—but only in a way that must be put through the grid of spiritual wisdom—how can the dream be treated as God's speaking? Ryle cannot have it both ways, and I believe he ends up confusing God's people.

Some writers who believe in direct guidance from God tell Christians to clear their minds and to believe that if a particularly vivid thought jumps into their heads (if it is not immoral), it could well be the guidance they need from the Lord. But that method of decision making never appears in Scripture. Yes, God can put thoughts into our minds, but so can Satan. So can our own hearts. The only way we can tell whether a thought is from God is to bring it back to the true source of wisdom, God speaking in Scripture.

Other writers alert believers to look for unusual circumstances by which God speaks: to scan for "open" doors—circumstances that offer little resistance to (and even invite) a certain course of action. The problem with this is that virtually no one would have done anything in the service of God had they guided their ministries by that principle. Noah would not have built the ark, Moses would not have faced Pharaoh, Joshua would have not marched around Jericho, etc. Again, these teachers cannot have it both ways. If God speaks, we need to listen, period. If God has already spoken everything he is going to say, then our focus should be on understanding and applying to our lives what he has said—not filtering circumstances to see if God is speaking through them.

These contemporary writers don't encourage but do usually tolerate what is called "putting out fleece." As we saw in chapter 6, this practice involves setting up a test (trap?) for God. We decide that if such and such an event happens, God is telling us to take some specific action (such as buy a house, marry a certain person, or enter full-time Christian service). While this method (and others like it) was used in the Old Testament, it was only approved as a test devised or approved by God, not by human beings.

While God may be gracious and submit to tests we wrongly devise, we surely should not test God in such a way. Most "fleecing" is used when there is an air of desperation (that is, unbelief) in the situation. Knofel Staton comments accurately on this practice:

> In biblical times signs were usually given because people did not believe, not because they did. . . . Are we any different? If God would come in person and tell us what to do in daily decisions, it might not make as much difference as many people think it would. You see, He did come in person in Christ and many did not believe. (Staton 1968, 38)

To be sure, Scripture describes many occasions when God spoke and led in all kinds of different ways. He spoke in visions, burning bushes, pillars of fire, donkey's mouths, and still small voices, as well as through the Urim and Thummim, angels, and foreign conquerors.

We mentioned some of these in chapter 2, but we can't assume that they are a pattern for us unless Scripture holds them out to us as such. Paul, for instance, struck the false prophet Bar-Jesus blind when he resisted Paul's preaching (Acts 13:9–10), but that is not a mandate for us to seek to blind those opposing the gospel.

Far too often, the claims of some that God led them by inner impressions, vivid thoughts, inner voices, dreams, unusual circumstances, and "fleecing" have crowded out the overwhelming biblical emphasis on our need to acquire godly wisdom and discernment. This result is a clear testimony to the unhealthy nature of this preoccupation. In most churches, one gets more respect by saying that "God told me" something than by sharing an application of God's values to your life. Jesus tells us to judge a teaching by its fruit (Luke 6:43–45) and the fruit of this sort of guidance has been very mixed. It often winds up associating the name of Christ with ridiculous decisions taken by unwise Christians—especially leaders hard up for credibility or cash.

A More Glorious Ministry

A deeper problem with these other methods is that they move us back to a spiritually deprived time in the history of God's work. We're taken back to the time before Christ came to earth as the incarnate image of God, before he came to live within us in the power of the Spirit. While we may be moved by the dramatic Old Testament stories of God's acts of revelation and deliverance, they pale next to the drama and power of the full revelation and cosmic deliverance the Son of God brings to earth in the final age of the Spirit.

We may wish that the Urim and Thummim were available today, or that we had prophets to tell us what God expected in our particular situations. But instead, God, in the person of the Holy Spirit, has come to dwell geographically within the body and heart of believers—both individually and corporately. Through the work of the Spirit in us, the words of God are internalized in our hearts and minds (Ezek. 36:26) in a way that Old Testament believers only dreamed about. Even the prophets longed to look into what God has revealed to us (1 Peter 1:10). Paul reflects on the superiority of the new age in Christ:

> *Now if the ministry that brought death, which was engraved in letters on stone, came with glory, so that the Israelites could not look steadily at the face of Moses because of its glory, fading though it was, will not the ministry of the Spirit be even more glorious? If the ministry that condemns men is glorious, how much more glorious is the ministry that brings righteousness! For what was glorious has no glory now in comparison with the surpassing glory. And if what was fading away came with glory, how much greater is the glory of that which lasts. (2 Cor. 3:7–11)*

In Old Testament times, the people related to God (with certain exceptions) as servants to a master (John 15:14). They received laws and detailed prescriptions for the course of their lives without necessarily understanding the overall plan. There was a greater degree of external discipline necessary to support faithfulness to God. While the Holy Spirit was active in the Old Testament, the redemptive gift of the Holy Spirit had not been given to believers.

But Jesus changed all that. We saw how, in two stages, he revealed everything the Father gave to him. He exposed the mystery hidden from the foundation of the world. Now it is ours, and with the giving of the Holy Spirit, we function as friends of God's, privileged to know his very mind and heart.

Given such wonderful developments, methods of guidance can never go back to the situation before the giving of the Spirit. Nor should we want them to! The days of the Urim and the Thummim are gloriously over. We are now sons and daughters, making decisions as the Father would make them himself. We are his representatives and ambassadors. We are like children who have attained adulthood and are entrusted with the wealth of the Father. Let's not adopt guidance models that move us back to a time of spiritual infancy! Let's rather hold out the full riches of our friendship with God, our Shepherd and Brother.

Pray that God may "fill you with the knowledge of his will through all spiritual wisdom and understanding" (Col. 1:9). Pray that as you look out at your life, your ministry, your family, friends, finances, time demands, and your world in all its need and future prospects, you would look at it through the eyes of Christ. Pray that you by his Spirit would be able to see from his perspective, keenly aware of the glory and character of the Father, all the values of God's kingdom, the reality of his enemy, and the priorities of the times.

For Review and Reflection

1. According to Colossians 1:10, how does one come to know the will of God?

2. What results from that knowledge of God's will?

3. According to Ephesians 5:15–17, what is the key to making the most of every opportunity and knowing the will of God?

4. To what extent is the goal of attaining spiritual wisdom highlighted in your church or Christian circles? Why do you think this is the case?

5. What does James 3:17 imply about the character transformation experienced by those who receive wisdom?

6. How is wisdom from heaven different from earthly wisdom?

7. In what ways is attaining wisdom more miraculous than receiving prophetic guidance?

CHAPTER

EXPERIENCING GUIDANCE

WE have seen that the New Testament presents a new and more miraculous model of God's guidance. God guides us by progressively placing within us spiritual wisdom and understanding to know the will of God. He no longer simply dictates his will to us. He never leads us with a "guess the signs" model. Rather, he offers us the understanding model.

But how do we experience this? What is it like for God to reveal his will through such discernment? I would suggest at least six experiences that qualify as guidance. There could be more, but in this chapter we will focus on six ways that God reveals his will through our understanding.

Specific Compassion

First, the Holy Spirit guides by focusing our hearts to love and serve specific people in specific ways. We cannot love or care for everyone (though we may have a heart to do so), so the Holy Spirit helps us to love our neighbor by laying specific situations upon our hearts and stirring us up to serve, show compassion, or minister to specific people. The Lord graciously links those people and situations to the values of Scripture and the character of God.

For example, Jesus enjoyed the guidance of the Father as he prayed all night before choosing the twelve disciples. God put a specific vision and burden upon Paul the apostle to minister to the Gentiles and to preach the gospel at the center of world culture—Rome.

God used a tent revival near Charlotte, North Carolina, to give Billy Graham a specific burden to preach the simple gospel to the lost. There are many other ministries that Dr. Graham could have potentially accomplished for God, but that is the one for which God granted him specific vision and compassion.

The Bible is full of references to the diversity of grace God gives to his body for different directions and roles in ministry. With each he gives a measure of faith to drive and empower its exercise. That faith registers in our consciousness as a specific compassion, vision, or conviction. This guidance is not a mystical, mind-bypassing experience. God connects the situation where the compassion is needed to the real biblical values of his kingdom and character.

Billy Graham saw a lost world under the judgment of God. His son, Franklin Graham, sees a slightly different world, where its peoples stand under both the judgment of God and the sufferings of poverty. That gives his ministry a somewhat different focus. But both father and son could wax eloquent about the objective biblical basis for their work.

Specific compassion can operate on a much smaller scale as well. My first experience of "guidance" involved compassion and conviction toward the young man walking behind me on the path home from school. I was not mystically drawn to him, but I had a convicting burden that this young man needed to hear the gospel. I know about the lost condition of everyone outside of Christ, but it is not God's will that I personally witness to every non-Christian. I believe the Holy Spirit made my values *specific* and *applied*. He connected the general command to preach the gospel to a concern for a specific person.

Specific compassion operates in a thousand small ways in the church and community life of God's people. I recall a dear young couple in the church I served as a very green pastor. They came to me and gave me a check for quite a few hundred dollars. They sensed (discerned) that my family had a need and they wanted to help us. They had been given the money by a parent and urged to take a cruise. They were moved instead to give it to us. At the time, we were just starting out in a mission church in a poor urban area, with a salary of $350 per month (in 1970). That gift not only helped us survive, but it was used by God to encourage us deeply in the work. God guided that young couple to fulfill the general biblical command to love by focusing on us.

Discerning Priorities

Second, God guides us by helping us identify priorities. Just as God allows us to see into the world with biblical and specific compassion, he also helps us *distinguish* what is important in specific situations in the light of God's values. He gives us the wisdom to know how to seek first the kingdom of God—the ability to look at life from the perspective of the unseen, eternal realm.

For instance, Paul the apostle was determined to go to Jerusalem to demonstrate his support for Jewish Christians who wanted to maintain their traditional temple practices and worship. Those he met along the way pleaded with him not to go, knowing that he could be killed. Prophets, in fact, foretold this. Yet Paul saw the critical priority of having this witness to the Jewish Christians and thus determined to go, rather than continue his very fruitful ministry to the Gentiles. God gave Paul an understanding of what was at stake in this specific situation. He enabled Paul to see the priority of defending the Jews' freedom to maintain their traditions. It was the will of God.

Struggling with God's priorities in different situations is the kind of guidance I seek most frequently. I am a fairly low energy person and often find myself without the strength or time to do everything I envision doing. (I am comforted to hear that high energy, Type A people also suffer from this!) After I've been enthusiastic about a few too many endeavors, the day of reckoning comes and I must choose what is most important in the light of eternity.

We all face priority decisions about the commitments we are asked to make; about balancing time with spouse versus children and work; about major purchases, educational investment in our children, etc. Many times God has graciously granted understanding about what my priorities must be, and I have grown as a result. I hope I have learned as well from those occasions when I have gotten it wrong.

Either way, it is comforting to know that God is teaching me how to apply his priorities to specific life situations. Knowing that he is behind that growth process is powerful motivation to learn to "be very careful, then, how you live—not as unwise but as wise, making the most of every opportunity, because the days are evil" (Eph. 5:15–16).

Moral and Spiritual Insight

A third way God guides us through discernment is through moral and spiritual insight. Insight is often mentioned in Scripture in association with wisdom. Wisdom tends to be evidenced in our actions, and insight refers to the ability to see into people, teachings, and situations.

First Kings 4:29 says that God gave Solomon "wisdom and very great insight." Because God promises insight, Paul tells Timothy to reflect on what he has written. If he does, Paul is certain that "the Lord will give you insight into all this" (2 Tim. 2:7). In 1 John 2:27, John reminds his readers that the work of the Spirit can give them an understanding of Christ that will enable them to remain in him—rather than defect to the false teachers.

In Philippians 1:9–10, Paul prays that the Philippians' love would "abound more and more in knowledge and depth of insight, so that you may be able to discern what is best and may be pure and blameless until the day of Christ." Notice that this insight operates in the area of "what is best." It enables believers to identify not just minimal right and wrong (prohibitions) but what is fitting, best, edifying, and most glorifying to God.

My most dramatic experience in this area of my life took place as I sat in a seminary apologetics class under the teaching of Cornelius Van Til. (Those of you who are not philosophy buffs will have to excuse this example.) I had come to seminary primarily to decide whether or not the God of the Bible was real. I peppered Dr. Van Til and others with questions for seven months. I had prayed (ironically) that God would reveal himself to me. After seven months of this, I asked Van Til if he believed in the "correspondence theory of truth" (the belief that apart from God one can demonstrate a correspondence between ideas/perceptions and objective reality). He said three words that changed my life: "Of course not." He reminded me that our confidence in the existence of truth does not rest in our philosophically proving a particular theory of knowledge. Christians believe it rests in the perfect and exhaustive knowledge God has of reality. "True human knowledge corresponds to *the knowledge which God has of himself and his world*" (Van Til [n.d.], 1).

I finally saw why it was consistent and necessary to begin with God in order to end with him. God took months to prepare me for this moment, but suddenly our glorious dependence on him for the certainty of knowledge became clear and alive to me. *I got it!* I repented of my philosophical assumption of human autonomy and embraced God afresh. I experienced deep Christian joy for the first time in my life, which washed away the existential depression that had characterized my previous two years. This was not mystical guidance or a dose of spiritual Valium. It was deliverance from a form of (pardon the expression) post-Kantian rationalism, though it had profound emotional reverberations for me. It transformed my view of God, which transformed my view of reality. In this form of guidance, God took the blinders off my eyes to give me spiritual insight into the truly self-existent and self-authenticating God.

God also answers prayer for insight into the unique design and giftedness of individuals. Romans 12:3 exhorts believers not to think too highly of themselves but to think soberly, as is fitting for a believer. Paul then gives some categories for understanding the gifts and roles of various members of the body of Christ. He lists prophecy, serving, teaching, encouraging, contributing, leadership, and showing mercy. Paul challenges believers in Rome to understand how they fit in the body of Christ. That takes insight.

When God commands us to do something (such as evaluate our gifts), he also helps us do it. He promises to grant insight to those seeking to use their gifts for him. This insight carries over into all that a believer does—including the use of his gifts at work. In fact, our labor is one of the primary ways we love our neighbor and do good (Eph. 6:8). In that arena as well, we should serve according to our gifts as much as we are able.

There are actually profound spiritual battles involved in serving according to one's design rather than for money, family approval, status, power, or recognition. I recently counseled with a Ph.D. scientist near the top of his research field who was asked to consider a new career as a manager of scientists—with significant increases in pay, prestige, recognition, and power. He sought the Lord for wisdom to know whether he had the gifts and design to take the job. God did guide him and gave him significant insight into himself and how he could best serve his company, his church, and his family—for the Lord's glory. I believe God delights in giving such insight to those who seek it.

Husbands need insight into their wives if they are to live with them in an understanding way (1 Peter 3:7). Elders and deacons need wisdom to lead God's people (Acts 6:3). Parents need insight into children so as not to discourage them but nurture them positively (Eph. 6:1–2). Leaders need wisdom to decide disputes in godly and fair ways (1 Cor. 6:5). Employers need insight and understanding regarding their workers to be fair and equitable as God commands (Eph. 6:9; Col. 4:1). We cannot love our neighbor, much less our enemies, unless we have understanding and insight into their thinking and the needs that link them to God.

In summary, we have seen in Philippians 1:9 that God grants insight when we desire to use it to serve and glorify him. We have a Savior who is full of wisdom and grace. He knows our hearts and, in calling us to follow him, has promised to guide us into that wisdom. He does this that we may serve as he did, fulfilling the work our Father sends us to do.

Words from God

A fourth way in which God may grant discernment is by helping us to know what to say. The Spirit may help us express our faith in Christ before the church or unbelievers. He helps us know what to say as we seek to witness to friends, exhort Christian brothers or sisters about their shortcomings, or encourage them in their walk. Ministers, Sunday school teachers, and Bible study and small group leaders who publicly handle the Word of God each week pray earnestly for this form of guidance. They are deeply aware of the way the Spirit gives them discernment into people's needs, applies God's Word to their situations, and enables them to communicate it effectively. First Peter 4:11 says, "If anyone speaks, he should do it as one speaking the very words of God."

God's promise to provide the right words is also presupposed in the New Testament expectation that believers will exhort, rebuke, encourage, and minister to one another, that husbands and wives will speak the truth in love, that parents will guide their children. The "one anothering" ministry is not optional; it is at the heart of personal ministry (Eph. 4:12; 5:16; Gal. 6:1–2; Heb. 10:25). This guidance does not come by the Holy Spirit taking over a person's speech center and speaking through the person like a ventriloquist through a dummy. Rather, the Spirit teaches and shows what should be said so that the speaker understands it and knows why she said it.

Led by the Spirit

Fifth, we experience guidance through being "led by the Spirit." This phrase occurs twice in theological passages—Galatians 5:18 and Romans 8:14. Paul's thought is the same in both passages but his development is fuller in Romans 8:13–16:

> For if you live according to the sinful nature, you will die; but if by the Spirit you put to death the misdeeds of the body, you will live, because those who are led by the Spirit of God are sons of God. For you did not receive a spirit that makes you a slave again to fear, but you received the Spirit of sonship. And by him we cry, "Abba, Father." The Spirit himself testifies with our spirit that we are God's children.

This passage gives assurance to God's children about their salvation. Paul assures us that if we, "by the Spirit" (see discussion on Gal. 5:16), are in a state of warfare with the sins of the fallen nature, we shall live. That is, we shall have eternal life. After emphasizing the active role of the believer, he complements it by referring to the active role of the Spirit. That brings him to say that "those who are led by the Spirit are sons of God" (Murray 1965, 295). Those who are led into battle by the Spirit are true Christians. The presence of the Holy Spirit creates a monumental warfare between our fallen nature and the Spirit-controlled "mind" (Rom. 7:25; 8:5–8).

Guidance in this sense is motivation for mortal conflict with sin and for godliness. As Christ was led (even driven) by the Spirit into the wilderness to face and defeat Satan, so we are led (even driven) by the Spirit into combat with the sin in our nature. We are assured of ultimate victory if we are willing to engage the enemy, which is, of course, the sin in ourselves. So if we are seeking the leading of the Spirit for our lives, we should be prepared for a different kind of leading than we might expect.

You will be "guided" to the conviction of sin and the need for God's grace. You will discover that there is nowhere to hide from the penetrating gaze of the Spirit. The Holy Spirit will identify the misdeeds of the body, work a deep hatred for sin, and a love-motivated desire to please God. We could call this experience guidance by moral motivation. God's children share his nature and character. They are therefore drawn toward their Father and away from the works of the sinful nature with all the power of their new nature. This leading of the Spirit is what creates our desire for the Father's love and leads us to cry "Abba Father."

The Internal Witness of The Spirit

A sixth but related guidance experience centers on what theologians call the "internal witness of the Spirit" (Rom. 8:16): "The Spirit himself testifies with our Spirit that we are God's children." This is an activity that seals "to the hearts of believers the promises which are theirs as heirs of God and joint-heirs with Christ and [generates] in them . . . the assurance of the great love the Father has bestowed upon them . . ." (Murray 1965, 298). The idea is not that the Holy Spirit issues a propositional verbal statement, "Thou art a child of God." What is promised is an internal sense of certainty and assurance. Our spiritual eyes are opened to sense the reality of our union with God through Christ. It is the experience of the love of God (Rom. 5:5).

In the same way, Peter emphasizes that this illumination of the unseen is worked in us through suffering. After describing the redemptive and purifying effects of suffering, he states its final result as follows: "Though you have not seen him, you love him; and even though you do not see him now, you believe in him and are filled with an inexpressible and glorious joy, for you are receiving the goal of your faith, the salvation of your souls" (1 Peter 1:8–9). This assurance cannot function unless we are resting on the promises of the gospel; it cannot be reserved on a shelf for the occasion when we may decide we can't trust the gospel message or want to enjoy a season of sin. Yet for those who are in Christ, it is the most valuable guidance work the Spirit ever accomplishes in our lives. It covers the issue of our eternal destiny; all other guidance pales in comparison.

This "internal witness of the Holy Spirit" is essentially the Holy Spirit personalizing and applying the truths of the gospel to an individual. It witnesses to me that I am a child of God. It goes beyond convincing me that God does indeed save people by his grace. Rather, it is the conviction that all that grace applies to *me*.

The Final Personalization

In many ways the internal witness of the Spirit is an illustration of a broader pattern of the Spirit's work in guidance. It is the pattern of personalizing and particularizing the work of God to our lives. The Spirit takes the general truths of Scripture and applies them to our lives and situations. He not only convicts of sin when we engage in prohibited activities or attitudes, but he encourages and prods us to positive obedience and service. The Spirit knows our weakness (Rom. 8:26–27), our hearts, and our gifts. He prays for us because we do not know how (or what) we ought to pray, but he does. He "intercedes for the saints in accordance with God's will" (Rom. 8:27). What a comfort it is to know that the Holy Spirit intercedes for us exactly as needed, exactly according to the will of God!

Summary

Summarizing the role of the Spirit in divine guidance, we can say the following:

1. The Spirit illuminates the connection between God's Word and our lives.

2. He does this by personalizing and particularizing (applying) the will of God for us.

3. This work of the Spirit is offered by God in response to believing prayer over a lifetime.

4. The result of the Spirit's work is not so much a "message from God" as it is a provision of "discernment and wisdom" granted for specific situations and progressively built into believers as a character trait.

5. Though it is wisdom from God, it also becomes our wisdom. Therefore guidance can be looked at from two perspectives. From God's perspective it is a direct gift, supernaturally given by the Spirit. From our perspective, it is our renewed mind enabled by God to see as Christ sees. It is our wisdom, yet it is God's. It is Christ's mind, yet it is given to us as ours. Scripture sees it both ways and so should we.

A Final Visit with the House Sitter

Let's think back to the story of the house sitter who volunteers to do landscaping for the couple who left town without leaving explicit directions. We suggested three alternative strategies:

1. Guess what the owners might want, by using clues left around the house and piecing together what you hope was their plan. This strategy requires you to "try to discover the will of God."

2. Wait for a call from the owners and thereby take the guesswork

out of the project. Avoid doing the wrong work. For guidance, this strategy says, wait on the Lord for an unambiguous message. Don't try to figure it out!

3. Study who the owners are, their preferences and style, and develop a plan that reflects these things.

Which of these is closest to the biblical model?

I hope you can see by now why we must reject strategy 1. In that scenario, the house sitter must guess what is in the mind of the owners by the clues left around the house—not by understanding the homeowner or the fundamentals of landscaping. We have tried to show that looking for clues to God's plan is fruitless because he does not (for good reasons) reveal his plan to us, except to look back at our history. While we depend upon his providential plan to control our world, we cannot know it in advance.

The second strategy involves waiting for God to tell us what to do. That is better than strategy 1 for two reasons. First, it moves us away from guesswork and interpreting signs on such an important matter. Second, it relies on God's preceptive (or revealed) will and does not seek to know something that God has said he does not ordinarily reveal. But it fails the standard presented in Colossians 1:9–11 and similar passages, which say that we know the revealed will of God *through spiritual understanding and wisdom*. God's will is given to us not by revelation (immediately) but by illumination (mediately). The Holy Spirit illuminates our understanding to grasp the things of God and apply them to our lives.

Therefore strategy 3, the wisdom model, is closest to how we find the will of God for our lives. In this strategy, the house sitter studies landscape design books in the owners' home, reads their journals (with permission!), and gets to know their personalities. He then designs a landscape he believes they will like. His work becomes a gift reflecting the depth of his knowledge of them. It turns out (continuing to use and stretch this parable) that the homeowners knew the house sitter quite well and were knowledgeable in landscape design themselves. In fact, they believed they knew well in advance what the project would look like when it was completed. The house sitter, in short, fulfilled their plan, but through his own wisdom.

Seeking God's will in this way involves us in a lifelong quest to grow in wisdom as we seek to honor and glorify God in the decisions we make. We seek wisdom from God in believing prayer and cultivate it as a primary life goal. We do this so that we might walk worthy of the Lord in every way and bear fruit in every good work (Col. 1:9–10).

For Review and Reflection

1. Can you give an example of a time when God guided you by granting you a specific compassion, vision, or burden?

2. What insights has God given you about the priorities you should have among competing demands in your life?

3. Can you identify moral and spiritual insights God has given you when you have faced important situations or decisions? Describe the insights.

4. Has God ever given you words to minister or witness in tense or difficult situations? Give an example.

5. What does the phrase "led by the Spirit" refer to in the Romans and Galatians passages? Describe the experience of being "led."

6. What is the internal testimony of the Spirit, and why is it so important to the believer? How is it a good example of the Spirit's work of guidance?

7. Which of the three views of guidance do you most identify with in the parable of the house sitter?

8. Has reading this book helped you identify guidance experiences that you had not previously recognized?

10

CHAPTER

PROVIDENCE:
THE LEFT HAND OF
GOD'S GUIDANCE

WE have seen that the Spirit guides us by illuminating God's will over a vast area of life. That is guidance with a capital G—the "right hand" of God's guidance. We could also call it "guidance proper."

But we have also seen that guidance proper does not cover circle 3, although it justifies everything in the circle. On some matters, God has not established a preference between one good and moral option and another. In those cases, he has given us a freedom and responsibility in decision making. Theologians call this the area of our Christian liberty. This area is controlled by God's providence (his preset, ordained plan), not his moral revealed will. Yet this providential control can still exert a strong, indirect guiding force on our lives. Therefore, we can look at this kind of providential control of circumstances as an indirect form of God's guidance, the "left hand" of guidance, or maybe guidance with a small "g."

I may, for instance, plan a fishing trip for a particular weekend, only to discover that a major hurricane is due to hit the spot I had chosen and evacuation is ordered. Plans are cancelled—because of God's providential "interference." After hearing the weather forecast, I can comfort myself that the trip was not supposed to have happened and that this was God's will (i.e., his plan). This is not guidance mediated through God's work of wisdom but through his direct control of circumstances outside myself. I am constrained by it, but I know it comes with the plan (or at least permission) of my God. So the Christian who knows God cares can call this kind of direction "guidance with a small g" or the "left hand" of God's guidance.

Obviously, events that happen in the providence of God can have a profound bearing on human plans. Providential action can shut them down (my fishing trip) or dramatically prosper them (the Normandy invasion in 1943, McGwire's seventy home runs). God's providence can also modify human plans (you are late because your car wouldn't start; your budget changes because your daughter tells you she plans to marry; or someone dies and leaves you a sizeable bequest). These are all ways that God's providential control can force change in our plans (see James 4:17). Our confidence is in the fact that "in all things God works for the good . . . [that we might] be conformed to the likeness of his Son" (Rom. 8:28–29).

God's providential control can include cancelling or altering plans we believed were his will. I might be stricken with a heart attack on my way to be installed as pastor of a church. I can be in a serious car accident on my way to share the gospel with someone. When we are doing the will of God, following what we believe to be his guidance, we can boldly pursue that goal, while realizing that it is finally subject to God's sovereign permission. Remember Paul's statement to the Romans that *if God willed,* he would come and visit them (Rom. 1:7).

Yet there is a danger in using the word *guidance* to describe God's providence. The danger is in trying to deduce God's moral (preceptive) will (what we should do) from his sovereign will (what actually happens). For instance, a family member who opposes a marriage might conclude that if the bride gets sick on her wedding day, it is God guiding her not to marry. Is this true? Not necessarily. Or perhaps someone is wondering whether to buy a new car until he finds out he won a $5,000 prize in a sweepstakes. Does that mean God is guiding him to buy the new car? Not necessarily. The actions of God's providence are not explained to us; they are part of his own sovereign plan (see chap. 3).

The New England Puritans struggled with this issue. They had reacted to the rationalism of the Anglicans by trying to read God's mind and will for New England into current events. Michael Winship discusses this phenomenon as it is illustrated in a sermon by Cotton Mather.

> Mather's sermon presented the classical Puritan vision of a communal social order dedicated to piety and reformation. He still had faith in the organic nature of society and in its ability to come to a consensus about what message God spoke to that society. He has no less faith in his place as an oracle for the community, reading for it the signs of the times and encouraging it to understand the message of those signs. (Winship 1996, 76)

The Puritans were tempted to cross the line from believing in the human and fallible interpretation of events to the belief that they were self-interpreting messages delivered by the ministers—just as the prophets delivered the messages of Jehovah in days of old. They sought to bind their community together by giving divine sanction to their particular view of what God was doing.

For example, most Puritans believed that God had publicly judged Ann Hutchinson for her heretical views when she gave birth to a child with severe birth defects (Winship 1996, 38). In so doing, they were making providence into revelation. This cannot and should not be done. They are totally separate acts of God and any connections made in human wisdom are speculative at best.

Jay Adams, a man well known to many in the field of Christian counseling, illustrated it this way (Adams 1996). He reminds us that circumstances are not like cans of sardines. When you are out camping and forget the can opener, it will be very difficult to get the food out of the cans you brought. Many of us have memories of trying to open a can of beans by beating it to death! Not so with cans of sardines. They come with a key attached and opening them is a simple matter. But circumstances are not like cans of sardines; they do not come with their own key by which we may interpret them. Providential circumstances require an outside key, held only by God. Human beings can only interpret events when the clear revelation of God applies.

However, God's providential care for his children affects guidance issues in another way. As the book of James puts it, "The prayer of a righteous man is powerful and effective" (James 5:16). Prayer changes things!

Many a saint has cried out for help from God and received it in a way that altered the course of his or her life (Heb. 4:16). The context of James 5:16 is prayer for the sick so that they would be healed. That is certainly a life-changing response from God! Others have asked for help with decisions totally outside the area of God's precepts and in the area of Christian liberty. God invites us to approach boldly for help in time of need!

We've already spoken of battlefield commanders who plead for help in making decisions that would spare the lives of their troops and enable them to win the battle. People who need important information *ought to* cry out to God, who can bring to their minds the answer needed (as he did for my grandfather in chap. 7).

God also (out of pure grace and compassion) occasionally submits himself to schemes concocted by more enterprising guidance seekers—such as setting up tests by which God is "forced" to show his hand and direction. "Lord, if you want me to go XYZ college, make their response letter be the first one." How about this one: "Lord, if I should invest in ABC Widget company, make the stock go down today." While this is a form of "testing" God that is forbidden in Scripture (Matt 4:7), it is all too commonly practiced by uninformed Christians.

While we all agree that testing God is wrong (unless God devises the test), what do we think of people reporting voices, hunches, dreams, impressions, and sensations that help them make decisions—decisions that are in the areas of wisdom guidance and Christian liberty? They provide dramatic stories of answers to prayer. Sometimes they do not pray at all; they just have an experience that helps them make a decision or take a direction.

Most Christians today want to say that these phenomena are part of how God reveals his will for our lives. However, this creates a bit of a paradox. On the one hand, they must accept these experiences as potentially valid revelations of God's will; on the other, they must put up some fences to keep bizarre and foolish outcomes from tarnishing the name of Christ.

Wisely, most try to solve this by saying that any direction gained through such experiences should be tested by a multitude of counselors, common sense, and the "does not contradict Scripture" criteria. The best writers on this topic, such as Dallas Willard, Blaine Smith, and Elizabeth Elliot, are especially strong in calling for caution.

Yet the irony is that the wisdom-based approach to guidance—rather than trying to protect our lives from the influence of impressions, hunches, dreams, and circumstances—allows us to enjoy them fully. We use them as *providential input*, not as *revelation* or spiritual guidance. The crucial difference is that they are *not* seen as a means of guidance. They are seen for what they really are: the workings of God's providence.

I'm sure you have had feelings about a decision that made you uneasy. You felt something was not right about it. That is a reason to focus more deeply on what is wrong, if anything. But the feeling is not the guidance! It is input that you received in God's providence, and it prompts you to further evaluation. Many times I don't feel right about something simply because it is a new way of doing things. *True guidance usually results in a "godly satisfaction" about a decision,* growing out of an effort to examine the issues prayerfully and come to a conviction.

In his daily governing of our lives, God can bring about circumstances, feelings, hunches, dreams, and other phenomena that suggest a course of action to us. We should evaluate that material as we would any ideas we received from any source—a friend, a news report, or a phone call. And we should evaluate it based on the revelation of Christ in the Word of God.

For example, recently I awoke too early to rise and begin my day, so I did some praying about upcoming events. I soon found myself meditating on how to organize a talk on wisdom. The talk was not flowing; it was wooden. Suddenly, in a flash, the idea came to me and I saw how to focus the presentation. I thanked God for the idea as his providential gift. I accepted it as mercy, not as guidance; as blessing, not revelation.

While we rejoice in the times that God deals with us in dramatic ways, we cannot assume that a dramatic burst of insight signals God's guidance. Satan also has access to our minds. He can and has planted many thoughts that occur with the same flash or vividness. God, Satan, our sinful flesh (Rom. 7:20), and our regenerate self (Rom. 7:25) all have access to our conscious mind.

These four sources can produce a storm of input to the believer. A sudden creative idea can be a provision from God or (as is often true in my case) an expression of my unrestrained enthusiasm for distractions to my calling in life. I am often "afflicted" with such vivid ideas after a good cup of coffee. Business owners often have a "stroke of genius" about a new product that can be a key to success or a tragic diversion from their core business. Unfortunately, as Adams pointed out, such ideas do not come with tags indicating whether or not they are help from God or plots of the Devil. You must evaluate the ideas on their own merit.

We must therefore put all such input through the grid of wisdom, discernment, and judgment. God desires us to do the hard work of bringing every thought captive to the lordship of Christ. Having the idea in a vivid or powerful way does not certify it as godly. Experiencing an amazing circumstance does not guarantee its divine origin. Ideas, thoughts, and circumstances are not self-authenticating—even ones that have no "rational" basis, such as a dream or prediction that may come to us.

In chapter 1 I related the vivid idea I experienced on my way home from school. It was just that: a vivid thought, a powerful idea. It did not by itself constitute God's guidance. It should not automatically compel me to wait for my schoolmate so that I could do what the thought beckoned me to do. However, the thought stimulated me to stop because I was convicted. The thought convicted me that I rarely think about opportunities to witness. I had recently been trained to share my faith and encouraged to try. Here was God's providence providing me an opportunity, and the Holy Spirit enabling me to make a connection with this particular young man. But the thought did not have some special "key" or trademark by which I could tell it was from God *apart from what I knew of God through his Word*. I believe that the connection between biblical principle and that specific boy made it real guidance.

Yet it was guidance, not revelation. In guidance God speaks, but it comes to me through my wisdom and discernment. It is subject to my limitations and biases, and my understanding can, therefore, be wrong. I must decide whether the thought is something God wants me to do. Therefore, using this wisdom model, I would never say to my schoolmate, "God told me to stop and witness to you." Such talk of God telling me to do something is usually motivated by fear, a desire to control the situation, or both. It is also very misleading in that it communicates to most people that I am receiving inspired and direct dictation from God. I am not. I should simply thank God that he convicted me to show love to this young boy. And I do thank him, because I need God's help to internalize this value even today.

For Review and Reflection

1. In what sense does God's providence guide us?

2. How does providential "guidance" differ from wisdom guidance?

3. Give some examples of providential guidance in your own life.

4. What caution is necessary in using the word guidance to refer to God's control of our life circumstances?

5. In the camping illustration, how are circumstances unlike the can of sardines?

6. How does wisdom-based guidance deal with dreams, hunches, and unusual circumstances that may seem to relate to needed guidance?

11

How to Become Wise

KNOWING that God guides through wisdom and understanding is the first step in actually enjoying that guidance. Such knowledge motivates us to seek wisdom so that we will know the will of God. But how do men and women become wise? Fortunately, there is abundant biblical teaching on that very topic, including the entire book of Proverbs. Let's turn to that question now.

To Get It, You Must Have It

Paradoxically, the Bible says that to become wise, you must already *be* wise. It takes wisdom to grow in wisdom. This sounds like a life-and-death "Catch-22." What's more, those who do not have wisdom (fools) will never be able to attain it—they do not have the foundation for becoming wise themselves. Both wisdom and foolishness are self-replicating and self-reinforcing. Wisdom by its very nature will increase itself in the one who possesses it, for she will recognize its value and seek it (Prov. 1:5). The fool, by contrast, believes he already possesses enough knowledge. He despises the humiliation of seeking correction or wisdom from another source (Prov. 1:22–33; 26:12).

The more wisdom you possess, the more you see your need, and so the more you seek. The more foolish you are, the less you see your need, and the more resistant you are to submitting to wisdom's teaching. Instead, you mock it and flee from it.

To darken the picture further, humanity (you and I included) in its natural state is born foolish. Proverbs says, "Foolishness is bound up in the heart of a child" (Prov. 22:15). Romans 3:18 caps its description of human depravity with the truth that "there is no fear of God before their eyes." Yet we know that the fear of the Lord is the beginning of (basis for) wisdom. It is the seed from which all other wisdom grows, and yet that seed is lacking in every child ever born upon earth—except one.

The good news of the gospel is that God sent Christ to break the "Catch-22." He came to make atonement for the sins of the world. He entered the pride and foolishness of our hearts to turn on the light of God. God's law convicts us, showing us our sin and pride. Christ convinces us to cast our sin upon him, that he might give us his righteousness and put his Holy Spirit within us.

That process of calling upon Christ for mercy and salvation is the transformation of a fool's heart into a wise man's. In fact, Paul the apostle says in 1 Corinthians 1:30 that Jesus Christ "has become for us wisdom from God—that is, our righteousness, holiness and redemption." He, Christ, has become our wisdom. When we embrace him, we have embraced the foundation and fountain (Col. 2:2; Prov. 8:1) of wisdom itself. In the same vein, Paul reminds Timothy that his mother taught him the message of the Scripture, which was able to make him "wise for salvation through faith in Christ Jesus" (2 Tim. 3:15). The very act of repenting and trusting in Christ for salvation is only possible because God is teaching you the fear of the Lord—the beginning of wisdom.

If you have bowed the knee to Christ and trusted him for salvation, you can become wise, reflecting the very wisdom of God. You may be young and inexperienced; you may have strayed far from God; you may be addicted; you may be poor and disrespected; or you may have led an outwardly respectable life while on the inside you have been a casket of moral rottenness. Whoever you are, wisdom can and will be yours if you are Christ's. The blessings and fruits of wisdom will come to you if you persevere under the loving discipline of God's care.

If you have not submitted your heart to Christ as your Savior from sin and the Lord of your life, you must begin there or remain in a state of self-perpetuating foolishness. It is the fool who says in his heart (or lives as if) there is no God to whom all are responsible. But those who lack wisdom are invited, solicited, and begged in Scripture to stop and listen to wisdom as she cries out on the street corner (Prov. 8:1–11). Everyone in *any* condition is invited to turn and listen and become wise. Christ came for such as you and me—as we see our need.

Once we have received Christ and repented of our sin, we can begin to enjoy a progressive, self-reinforcing growth into wisdom, insight, and discernment. Let's look more specifically at how God works this wisdom in the disciple's life.

Progressive Consecration to God

Once converted, the second step for the Christian is to open his or her heart progressively to who God is—as opposed to the false gods we naturally serve and fear. Our conversion to God occurs at a single point in time, but our conversion is also the dramatic beginning of a process in which we consciously consecrate more and more of our hearts to God. The path of wisdom is a lifestyle of repentance from serving functional gods like security, safety, control of situations, pleasure, power, ease, avoidance of pain, and approval. God will systematically expose any such rivals in our hearts that divert us from loving and worshiping him. We must be prepared for that and even search out such duplicity in our hearts.

One clear sign of a wise person is that he accepts rebuke and discipline from God. Proverbs 1:23 says,

Chapter Eleven

If you had responded to my rebuke,
I would have poured out my heart to you
and made my thoughts known to you.

Solomon urges his son,

Do not despise the LORD's discipline
and do not resent his rebuke,
because the LORD disciplines those he loves,
as a father the son he delights in.
(Prov. 3:11–12)

When you are discovered in a sin by a parent, spouse, coworker, or fellow Christian, how do you ultimately respond? Do you resent God's providence? When you experience the consequences of your own folly, do you blameshift or become fatalistic or bitter? A person who desires to become wise listens, learns, and ultimately thanks God for correction—even through the painful exposure of heart evil.

As George Schwab points out in his excellent article, "Proverbs and the Art of Persuasion,"[1] "Proverbs' target, anthropologically speaking, is the 'heart.' The word occurs ninety-four times in Proverbs" (Schwab 1995, 8). Dr. Schwab expounds the truth that the heart is a religious organ and that from it proceed the issues of wisdom and folly, life and death. Another excellent resource on developing a heart that fears the Lord (as the antidote to all other fear) is Edward Welch's book, *When People Are Big and God Is Small.*[2] It is appropriately subtitled *Over-*

---

1 This article is one of the most biblically astute treatments of how Proverbs seeks to change people. Schwab contrasts it with the psychotherapeutic approach and finds a stark contrast.
2 Phillipsburg, N.J.: P&R Publishing, 1997. Published in cooperation with the Christian Counseling and Educational Foundation, Glenside, Pa.

coming Peer Pressure, Codependency, and the Fear of Man. Dr. Welch takes a penetrating but redemptive look at how the dynamics of heart idolatry infect and influence our lives. He shows how the work of Christ liberates us from such folly, emptiness, and addiction to truly worship God from the heart.

Such heart recognition and fear of God will produce a sure growth in wisdom. Such growth is now open to all of us who are in Christ—as we allow him to cleanse and renew our hearts to love God alone.

You Must Seek It

The third thing we need to grow wise, Proverbs tells us, is to want wisdom enough to pursue it consistently. We must find it, listen to it, and take it in. We are urged to pursue it more diligently than silver or gold. That is quite a challenge in a world where education seems oriented to obtaining the silver and gold of a big paycheck.

> *Lay hold of my words with all your heart;*
> *keep my commands and you will live.*
> *Get wisdom, get understanding;*
> *do not forget my words or swerve from them.*
> *Do not forsake wisdom, and she will protect you;*
> *love her, and she will watch over you.*
> *Wisdom is supreme; therefore get wisdom.*
> *Though it cost all you have, get understanding.*
> (Prov. 4:4–7)

This is one passage of many (in both Testaments) that offer wisdom to those who seek it diligently (see James 1:5).

We have defined wisdom as the moral ability (both the skill and the understanding) to apply practically the character and purposes of God to your life. The person seeking wisdom is motivated in the following ways: She is a person who wants to reflect God in all she does (Rom. 12:1–2). He is a person who prays for wisdom to know God's will (Col. 1:9–11) so that he might do it in the real world (James 1:22–25). She is a person who meditates on the written Word of God, seeking to internalize and appropriate its truth (Pss. 1 and 119) for her life. God has graciously laid out such counsel for all of us in the book of Proverbs. Those of us who may have had fathers or mothers or youth leaders or relatives who were not wise need not despair. We can learn not only from the providential discipline of the Lord, but directly from his own mouth.

Further, because of this genuine heart motivation for God, the person who seeks wisdom maintains that desire. He perseveres because he believes that God will honor his promise to grant it (Prov. 2:1–5). Therefore, he does not give up in the midst of sin, defeat, or confusion. He accepts cleansing, holds solidly to his hope in Christ, and continues seeking God to give light. The person growing in wisdom does not "revert" to other gods, short-cuts, or folly when the true God does not meet his timetable or expectations. He waits for the Lord. He does not settle for false wisdom—cleverness, manipulation, or power, escape, intimidation, or other forms of the "wisdom that is from below" (James 3:13–18). In short, the person seeking wisdom from God makes it a life prayer and pursues it from God unconditionally.

Associate with the Wise

The fourth step to growing in wisdom is to seek it not just from God but from those whom God has provided. Proverbs itself is structured as the wisdom of a wise and godly father to a son. It emphasizes that the wise man (as opposed to the fool) values correction, discipline, and rebuke. The fool rejects correction and mocks those who try to give it. The wise man listens to his parents and those God has put in his life to advise him. He not only listens to them but seeks out their counsel and the counsel of the godly.

Becoming a new creature in Christ means that you will now need to enter this new lifestyle of pursuing wisdom. You will need to learn from others how to live out the character and purposes of God. Men and women of godly wisdom are placed by God within the church to help you grow; to help you walk worthily of the Lord in your marriage, personal life, parenting, job, and ministry. They can be of immense help to you because of God's promise to bless the transfer of wisdom across spiritual generations (from the spiritually mature to those less mature in the Lord).

How often do we ask faithful men and women for an evaluation of what they see in our lives? Do we ask where they see us as compromised, unfruitful, falling short of God's way, neglecting priorities or opportunities? Do we pursue those who have the wisdom and position to help us see ourselves against the backdrop of God's character? Or do we just wait and hope that nobody criticizes us? Many of us live in quiet fear that someone will find out what we are really like. Others try and convince themselves that no one else knows enough about them (even spouses or parents) to tell them frankly their faults and encourage their growth in Christlikeness.

Most of us (particularly men) do not put ourselves in a position to receive that kind of feedback. Yet the "one-anothering" ministry of the New Testament and Proverbs is basic to the ability to reflect God in our lives. In my counseling experience, I find that men are usually dragged into counseling by their wives. However, once there, most Christian men respond well and benefit greatly because they do fear the Lord. They just have a barrier of fear, pride, and/or folly to overcome in the beginning.

I still remember a summer camp counselor who helped me in this way during my junior high years. By the end of my week at camp, I was very motivated to bring my life into conformity to Christ's. I remember being moved to go to my counselor and ask him what he saw in me: the good and especially the bad. I did not have that kind of direct openness with my father, and I still remember the deep joy at opening myself up to a wiser, godly man. It is interesting that I no longer remember what he said, except that he saw both good and bad. What I remember is the deeply strengthening way that my counselor came alongside me with life-giving counsel. God used that experience to motivate me to look for others who could function in that way. He has periodically blessed me with such people.

During the last four years of my twelve years as a pastor, my five elders functioned that way. We sensed that we were burning out with the stress of church leadership and sought counsel from Dr. Edmund Clowney, then President of Westminster Seminary. He challenged us to develop a spiritual fellowship among the elder board. We accepted the challenge and adopted a role of praying for and "one-anothering" each other. We allocated regular priority times of elder fellowship for that purpose. Outside of marriage, it was the most powerful fellowship I have experienced in my life, and I grew steadily as a Christian. I was one pastor who no longer felt alone. Incidently, by building that level of fellowship among the elders, we reduced the time needed for elder business by 50 percent.

That kind of wisdom-building fellowship can take place at many points in the life of a church: men's groups, women's groups, discipling groups, staff fellowship, youth groups, task-oriented ministry fellowships. Even properly run Sunday school classes can be the means for sharing wisdom. Proverbs 13:20 reminds wisdom seekers that "he who walks with the wise grows wise, but a companion of fools suffers harm." That principle brings up another concern in this age of unlimited media exposure.

Dr. Robert Hicks in his helpful book, *In Search of Wisdom,* warns against the potentially destructive effects of unwise media exposure.

> Today, these associations are not only the people we spend time with daily, but the associations we form in the artificial world of television and literature. What we read and watch have become far more powerful socializers than the real people we deal with. (Hicks 1995, 238)

For many of us, the hours spent immersed in newspapers and magazines, TV or cinema, are far more than we need for legitimate diversion or information. The inordinate pursuit of entertainment can easily compete with the pursuit of wisdom. Additionally, many media offerings can subtly reshape our Christian worldview into conformity with the values of this age. My own TV watching has, for example, rotated between the atheistic and evolutionary show *Star Trek,* the false "male religion" exhibited in outdoor shows, the secular priorities of the 6:30 news, and the great entertainment of college basketball. You can see that I have my work cut out for me—evaluating the (potential) effect these shows have on my life. I must remember Proverbs 14:8:

> *The wisdom of the prudent is to give thought to their ways,*
> *but the folly of fools is deception.*

(See also Eph. 5:15–17 and Rom. 13:11.)

Seek Specific Counsel

In the midst of a life that includes association with the wise, the person who seeks to become wise seeks (as a lifestyle) *specific* counsel for important decisions. Confusion, insecurity, fear, and even overconfidence are God-given opportunities to learn from wise men and women. Proverbs commends seeking advice on specific decision making (Prov. 15:22; 13:10; 11:14). Proverbs 19:20 promises that the habit of getting advice at specific points will spur the growth of wisdom as a character trait.

The life pursuit of wisdom coordinates with the continuing process of daily decision making. The particular decisions you must make are there by the providence of God. They are part of your long-term training in wisdom, as well as the occasion for God to provide specific wisdom for a specific decision. We cannot expect God to make us wise without being trained by the process of obedient daily decision making. We gain wisdom as we seek to exercise it.

For example, Olympic swimmers do not wait until they set a world record time in practice before they compete in swim meets. In the same way, the Christian must enter into the daily tests of decision making as part of the long-term process of becoming wise. God provides both specific decision-making wisdom *and* wisdom internalized as a character trait. Each reflects and deepens the other.

In summary, to become wise one must:

(1) know God and be changed by him,

(2) be committed to a progressive consecration to God,

(3) diligently and persistently seek wisdom,

(4) learn from those who are wise, and

(5) participate in the ongoing decision making God requires of us daily.

The focus of this chapter has been the development of wisdom as a character trait. It is a lifelong process that is part of the Holy Spirit's work of making us like Christ.

Part Four has a somewhat different focus—the specific decision-making challenges for which we seek specific guidance from God. What does it look like to actually implement all the principles we have considered thus far?

Chapters 12 to 18 are a case study illustrating the process of wise decision making in a specific, real-life situation, the story of Don and Glenda.[3] As the story unfolds, I hope that you will see how the seven elements involved in specific decision making are related to the five elements of long-term growth in wisdom we studied in this chapter. Each reflects and deepens the other.

For Review and Reflection

1. How would you describe the "fear of the Lord"?

2. Do you think you fear the Lord? If so, why?

3. Why is the fear of the Lord the "beginning" of wisdom?

4. Are wise people recognized and honored in our culture? How are they recognized in the church? How many people do you know that have the character quality of godly wisdom?

5. What would you look for in a wise man or woman?

6. What are the biggest obstacles to the development of wisdom in today's church and culture?

7. To what extent has wisdom been something you have sought?

8. How could you pursue it more persistently?

---

3 This case study is based on a true story but also includes elements from other actual cases to provide a broader coverage of issues that arise in real-life decision making.

Seeking Guidance:
The Seven Elements of
Biblical Decision Making

Don's Dilemma

Don is thirty-two and does not like his engineering job. He is married to Glenda and they have two children, five and eight. They are both committed Christians and active in their church. Glenda is a fairly new Christian. Don has worked in the field of civil engineering for eight years, and has gained considerable experience at his specialty —predicting and determining the effects of water runoff from various construction projects, particularly highways. His job is secure and is pretty much guaranteed lifetime employment. Glenda especially appreciates the security of that unspoken guarantee. Though "security-oriented," she is not withdrawn, but is very honest and forthright.

Don balks at seeking any advancement in the firm or in his field. He cannot seem to summon up the motivation or vision for even daily, routine tasks. He attributes these attitudes to his belief that if he is promoted, he will get further locked into a field where he is not happy. He says to himself, "How could I be so dense to study engineering for four years, spend a fortune of tuition, and put in eight years in a field I hate?" He asks himself, "Why did it take me so long to figure this out?" Glenda, on the other hand, is very thankful for his job because it is very straightforward, requires little or no overtime, and pays fairly well. She reminds Don that there are not many jobs that give a committed Christian the chance to do well in a profession and still have the time to be a father, husband, and active church member. She thinks Don's biggest problem is his attitude. Why can't he simply enjoy the job for which he is so qualified? Why can't he just be content? Don's parents wonder the same thing.

To complicate matters, Don and Glenda purchased a spacious home three years ago with the understanding that an increasing income would enable them to handle it financially. Now that Don seems to want out, he worries about how he will pay the mortgage, especially since the housing market has been flat since he bought it. It would be difficult to sell without taking a loss.

Everything, it seems, has conspired to keep him at his current job: wife, housing market, training, experience, security, parents, and even his boss (who gives him good reviews). Yet the detailed, boring, and seemingly irrelevant work in a large bureaucratic organization weighs on him more every day. Don has even considered making intentional mistakes or being late with work; this way, he reasons, he would avoid being offered a promotion and further trapped in the world of engineering. Yet, if he turns down a promotion, he will be locked in at his current salary for the rest of his life. Don knows that something has to change. But how? He needs guidance from God.

A friend sought to enlist Don in a multi-level marketing company. Another friend thought he would be a good manufacturer's rep and offered to help him get a pure commission sales job. But both these jobs seem too risky to Don and Glenda. He was trained as an engineer. How could he quit and start to work on pure commission with no guarantee that he would make the $50,000 he makes now? That's the minimum they need to make their house payments and send their children to Christian school. Therefore they turned down these "opportunities."

Glenda offered to go to work since their youngest had just entered kindergarten. That way Don could relax in his position as an engineer and not feel so much pressure to climb the ladder in a field he hates. She also thought that the extra money would help if Don changed jobs and began his new position at a lower salary. Don was deeply moved by Glenda's offer and reluctantly accepted it.

However, while driving around looking for work, Glenda was involved in a major car accident and injured her spine so seriously that she had to discontinue her plans to work. Don was overwhelmed. Now he had *more* pressure to make it as an engineer and provide for his partially disabled wife.

Let's follow Don as he seeks to apply the wisdom view of guidance to his dilemma. To do so, we will need to see the connections between Don's situation and God's will and preferences revealed in Scripture. This story will show you, "up close and personal," how the Holy Spirit actually shined his light on very spiritual issues in Don's life, directing him by understanding and spiritual wisdom—not by impersonal, mystical clues. We will also see the "left hand of guidance" (God's providence) and how it actually worked in this true story—and how it fit perfectly into God's total management of Don's life.

I believe that we can identify seven elements in wisdom-based decision making. They are *consecration, information, supplication, consultation, meditation, decision, and expectation.* These seven steps are not taught as a sequence in any one Scripture passage, but summarize what the Bible teaches in many places in many ways. These steps are not isolated from each other; they are all related. Some people may, therefore, divide them up differently. You can decide for yourself as we look at each of them. I offer these steps in a logical order, but they are rarely followed in any particular order in real life. However, I believe that these elements need to be part of every search for guidance from God. As you will see, there is some rationale for the general order of the steps.

12

CHAPTER

CONSECRATION

TO be led of God, we must belong to God. Romans 12:1–2 puts it beautifully:

> *Therefore, I urge you, brothers, in view of God's mercy, to offer your bodies as living sacrifices, holy and pleasing to God—this is your spiritual act of worship. Do not be conformed any longer to the pattern of this world, but be transformed by the renewing of your mind. Then you will be able to test and approve what God's will is—his good, pleasing and perfect will.*

Our essential (spiritual) worship is not singing hymns in church, but offering ourselves to God in gratefulness for his mercy. The sacrifice of ourselves means that we no longer pattern our lives after the motives and goals of this age, but exchange our old ambitions and ways of living for the new ones God has for us. It is the renewed mind that accepts the life goal of being an instrument of God's purpose. This consecration lays everything on the altar: job, spouse, children, money, the desire for security, power, influence, sexual pleasure, hobbies, sports, friends. These different areas of human life are not eliminated or given over in some act of dour penance and monastic resignation.

No, they are given to Christ in order to vitally join them to *his* powerful program for our lives and his purposes in the world.

They all now function under the lordship of Christ and are brought to life within his kingdom purposes. Jesus himself taught us in Matthew 6:33, "But seek first his kingdom and his righteousness, and all these things will be given to you as well." Jesus is making it clear that we must not attach ourselves to any of his blessings in this life. We must not seek our life there but rather in his renewing rule. We may have no other gods before him.

Remember our discussion of the "double-minded" man in James 1:7? God will not answer that man's prayer for wisdom because he is "double-souled," drawn in two directions, trying to serve both God and the world. To be guided by God into his will, we must lay our entire lives, our future, our bodily health, our personal happiness, our money, our relationships, and our goals all on the altar, and dedicate them to his purposes. That means basing our earthly lives on what he gives us back from the altar to be used for his glory.

The unconsecrated person seeks to use God's guidance to achieve his own goals. God is his servant, there to build his kingdom. That, of course, is the norm in pagan religious guidance. There is no real love for God or worship of a deity; instead there is a focus on appeasing them so that one's own goals could be achieved. That kind of religion is very much alive within each of our sinful hearts.

Is your experience like mine? I often cry out to God for guidance when I have taken a wrong turn and am in trouble. We assume self-sufficiency the rest of the time, though that self-sufficiency may not be obvious because we have publicly professed faith in Christ and are active in Christian service. When things are going well, we rarely remember even to thank him, much less to seek guidance from the Holy Spirit about pleasing him in our next steps. The Holy Spirit regularly has to convict and forgive us of our "success orientation," which rules our hearts in place of the "service orientation" that befits a redeemed rebel. I find that this is also typical of many of the men with whom I counsel. So many of us are goal-oriented. We convince ourselves that we have put everything on the altar, yet our motive for all that "sacrifice" is not God's glory. It is that a specific but unspoken and unconsecrated goal of ours might be achieved through God's help.

I see this frequently when I counsel pastors who have trouble in their marriages. These men are often willing to sacrifice everything, including their wives, to God, but it is for the purpose of securing God's blessing on *their* work. It is not a sacrifice out of a sense of God's mercy. It is not for God! It is a sacrifice in pursuit of a coveted goal— the blessing of God on *their* ministry. The parallels to men in nonministry work abound, but this syndrome can be hard to see because of the layers of falsely religious justification that hide its true character.

We rarely have the insight to see these goals because we cherish them more than God himself. Fortunately, Christ takes it upon himself to expose these idols, so that as he shines his light on them, we might also lay them down at his feet. When they are exposed, some men will repent with deep sorrow, but others will respond like the man who told me, "My ministry must come before my marriage." That man was on his way out of both his marriage *and* his ministry.

Let's consider Don and the consecration issues involved in his life.

Don and Consecration

Don had gone forward in a revival meeting and rededicated his life to Christ some twelve years earlier. He thought of himself as a consecrated Christian. However, when he began to be paralyzed with fear about his vocational future, he knew he had a problem. While it was obvious to Don (and a little bit, to Glenda) that engineering was not tapping into his motivations, he began to wonder if his passivity at work was rooted in something deeper—perhaps a form of sin. Was he protecting as sacred the idea that his job would be a source of life, giving fulfillment to him? When he experienced boredom, bureaucracy, and frustration, he felt as if his life was being suffocated. That, however, was what he usually experienced at work. He fantasized about a place where he could draw deep motivating power from the work environment.

For Don, the challenge of overcoming obstacles and experiencing "real life" victory gave him a sense of justification for this life. It created for him a tangible sense of his value. Calculating water runoff rates for highways was not Don's idea of personal vindication.

God graciously convicted Don through two or three probing discussions with his pastor. He had wisely gone to ask his pastor if he saw anything in his life that was inconsistent with Christ. The pastor pointed to some occasions when Don had complained about his "stupid" job to others in the church.

As they discussed the roots of this attitude, Don saw that he must actually "seek first the kingdom of God," not the self-actualization of a job that offered the drama of combat and victory. He acknowledged his idolatrous grasping after self-justification through work, and asked God for forgiveness and cleansing through the sacrifice of Christ. He dedicated that area of his life to Christ and determined to have the attitude of a servant. He was shocked to see the extent to which he had allowed his desire for self-actualization to displace his sense of dignity as a son of God, called to serve Christ in engineering and calculating water runoff.

Don also grieved. He was deeply aware of the amount of love God must have for him, to keep working with him despite his search for life apart from God. He remembered that Christ did not come to earth to seek self-justification or fulfillment: "The Son of Man did not come be served, but to serve, and to give his life as a ransom for many" (Matt. 20:28).

Based on that, Don determined that although he did not like his job, he would approach it as a servant each day he worked there. He committed himself to putting the energy of his love for Christ into the "dumb" projects he did, even if he could do them in his sleep. He tried to see his work as a grand battle between the idol of "emotional payoff" and the true God in whom he found his glory. There *was* a battle God wanted him to fight, not for his self-justification, but for the honor of God's name.

Don was also embarrassed when he remembered his prayers for guidance when taking the engineering job some eight years earlier. He thought to himself, "Here I am complaining about the job that I asked God to guide me into. I asked God and this was his answer. Now I am rejecting it. How can I ask God for future blessings if I have not been a good steward of his present provision?"

Don also noticed that once his expectations of self-fulfillment stopped ruling him, his mind began to clear from the coercive reign of fear. He could leave the future to God and focus his energy on the task at hand. He could think and pray creatively about alternatives and options. He knew he still wanted to find a way out of his situation, but he understood that his true life did not depend upon that. He could plan, pray, and look for God's answer in God's time. (He just hoped God would not delay too long!)

Glenda secretly hoped that Don's new-found consecration would result in a gradual return of happiness in his present job. She prayed that God would enable him to remain an engineer and use the training he had paid so much to receive. Neither she nor Don's parents could see why God would want him in another field.

In summary, the first step in seeking guidance from God is to ask him to test and search our hearts for any areas of life, beliefs, or motives that are not given over to him. Seek the help of your pastor or someone else who knows you well to explore possible hidden or unbiblical goals. As you discover them, confess them and receive God's forgiveness with thanksgiving. Then, seek new patterns of obedience, thought, and motivation.

God guides his own sheep. To the extent that we are giving ourselves over to the control of the world's blessings, we are not even seeking guidance from God. We are being led by the world even though we may profess to want the Spirit's leading. James 4:1–10 reminds us that anger, quarrels, and disputes coming from our frustrated goals are a sure sign of this phenomenon.

If, as far as you know your own heart, you have turned every area of your life over to Christ, and you are actively seeking to find your life in him, then you can know that you will find the "good, acceptable, and perfect will of God."

For Review and Reflection

1. According to Romans 12:1–2, how does consecration relate to finding the will of God?

2. How do you think consecration relates to our previous discussion (chap. 11) of having the "fear of the Lord"?

3. Have you ever sought God's guidance or help so that you could achieve an "unconsecrated goal"? What were your motives for seeking that goal?

4. What did Don want out of work that he should look to God to provide?

5. What was the biblical alternative to working for the "emotional payoff" Don sought in his job?

6. Have you ever acknowledged and repented of seeking such pay-offs? Did such consecration help you gain wisdom and perspective on the area of your life affected by that ungodly desire?

13

CHAPTER

INFORMATION

AFTER we have consecrated ourselves to God, we can begin seeking his specific guidance to help us in decision making. The place to begin is with the gathering of information.

That should not be surprising. We saw earlier that most of the situations where guidance from God is needed are ones where neither alternative is evil in itself. For example, in the decision between taking a job as a nurse in a hospital or a rehab center, neither option is bad in itself. It is the total situation (motivation, giftedness, freedom, etc.) that makes one choice best. Those are the specifics that a Christian decision maker is called to discover.

This is very different from a situation where our options include things that are prohibited by God. We do not need additional information, for example, to decide whether or not to participate in a fraudulent land deal. God's Word is clear. Yet I do need information to decide whether God would want me to witness to someone in the mall or return to my car, where my wife has been waiting for twenty minutes. Staying another twenty minutes to share Christ could be the wrong decision or the right one. It all depends on the specifics of the situation. Does my wife know where I am and what I am doing? Do I have her support for such a delay? What other commitments does *she* have?

While information alone (without principles) is never enough to provide guidance, gathering the information that God has made available is a critical component in godly decision making. We need information about ourselves, the others involved, potential consequences, responsibilities, and of course, circumstances. F. B. Meyer puts it well when he says,

> God has given us these wonderful faculties of brain-power and He will not ignore them. In grace He does not cancel the action of His marvelous bestowments but He uses them for the communication of His purposes and thoughts. (Meyer 1896, 12)

Let's turn now to some biblical examples of this critical component in decision making guided by God.

Information Gathering in the Bible

God created Adam and Eve with the ability to know and subdue the earth, and to fill it with their children (Gen. 1:28). Part of this task was to discover and classify the living creatures (Gen. 2:20). That required study, observation, and abstraction. This mandate continued despite the fall into sin and the resistance of the thorns and thistles that grew. Adam and Eve's rule involved the mastery of large amounts of information regarding the world they were called to subdue.

In another example of data gathering, God himself sent angels to investigate the wickedness of Sodom (Gen. 19:20). God's principles of judgment were clear to him, but he sent the angels to get the data on what category of judgment Sodom deserved, based on the specifics of the situation. Were the facts as bad as the "outcry" that had come up to God?

In another example, God commanded Moses to send spies into the land of Canaan to scout out the land.

See what the land is like and whether the people who live there are strong or weak, few or many. What kind of land do they live in? Is it good or bad? What kind of towns do they live in? Are they unwalled or fortified? How is the soil? Is it fertile or poor? Are there trees on it or not? (Num. 13:18–20)

God, of course, knew what the people were like, and he could have told Moses. But he wanted the people to see it for themselves. He wanted them to see that Canaan conformed to all that had been promised them as a land that flows with milk and honey. He also wanted the faith of the leaders to rest in God *in full view of the size and strength of the Canaanites*. He wanted the Israelites to say, "Yes, God will give us the land even though there are giants in it." They needed to see the giants, then believe that God would fulfill his promises.

God often deals with us in the same way. Our information gathering requires us to see with our own eyes the situation in which we must trust God and make decisions. He wants us to apply the promises of the Word to the situations we experience. Proverbs speaks about information gathering in Proverbs 18:17: "The first to present his case seems right, till another comes forward and questions him." In other words, we had better get both sides of any story before deciding our response to a solicitation or dispute.

In the New Testament, we see the apostle Paul adapting his ministry specifically to the situation of each church. He does not write the same letter to each one. In Corinth he had reports of specific problems which he addressed directly. He dealt with entirely different problems in Philemon, Colossians, and 1 Thessalonians. Each was based on knowledge of the situation gained from letters, personal reports, or individuals Paul had sent to see to their condition. The sheer diversity of these divinely inspired letters is testimony to the importance of the *specific situation* to which the eternal, unchangeable gospel is applied.

Chapter Thirteen

The apostle Peter commands husbands to "be considerate" (lit., "live according to knowledge") "as you live with your wives" (1 Peter 3:7). Just as the apostle Paul sought to understand his churches in order to minister to them, so Peter tells husbands to understand their wives, so they can properly respect and honor them. Husbands will not find this specific information about their wives in the Bible. They will have to do the hard work of listening and building up a knowledge of what "makes them tick." They must study their wives, their values, their responses, their needs, their goals, their weaknesses, and their strengths. No two wives are alike; each is unique. Living "considerately" will therefore be different for each one. Yes, to some extent the will of God will be "different" for each one.

Christians are also commanded to gather this kind of information on themselves. In Romans 12:3 Paul says, "Do not think of yourself more highly than you ought, but rather think of yourself with sober judgment, in accordance with the measure of faith God has given you." Here Paul is clearly commanding the careful gathering of accurate information about yourself. We are to use sober judgment to identify our gifts (see vv. 6–8) and our measure of faith (vv. 3, 6). This is critical information if we are to do the will of God as we serve him within the body of Christ. Unfortunately, our names are not listed in Scripture with our gifts identified. We must discern this information ourselves, with the help of God and others. We are commanded to assess both our gifts and our God-given motivation (faith) for the exercise of that gift. Both must be guiding forces in the development of our personal work and church ministry.

Don and the Information He Needs

Don needs help in gathering the right kinds of information about his situation. He began by identifying the key questions he would need to answer. Don and his pastor sat down and came up with this list:

1. What does not fit Don in his current employment? Is it biblical to change jobs because of a poor fit?

2. What strengths and motivations can Don invest in the workplace?

3. Which industries might offer opportunities for his abilities?

4. How much risk and stress could Glenda reasonably endure while Don gets established in his new job?

5. Under what conditions would Don move to another city and uproot his family?

6. What job titles should he apply for and with which companies?

Don told his pastor of his commitment to submit his work life to Jesus Christ. He explained that although he felt more at peace, he still struggled with his fear of being stuck in engineering for the rest of his life.

Don wanted his pastor's advice on whether it *mattered to God* what kind of work he did. Should he just learn contentment with engineering, or should he also seek a different kind of work? Don's pastor rightly advised him to do both. On the one hand, it is not necessary to change lawful occupations just because we are Christians (1 Cor. 7:17, 20). We can learn contentment in the situation to which God has called us. As long as we do not seek to draw from work what we should seek from our relationship with God, we will be able to learn contentment—even in a situation where we are "misfits." In fact, Don's pastor continued, God uses such situations specifically to build and test character in us (Rom. 5:3–5).

On the other hand, the pastor showed Don that he should always seek to make better use of the freedom and gifts God has given to him (Rom. 12:3–8). Paul advises singles to marry if much of their energy would otherwise be diverted into maintaining sexual purity (1 Cor. 7:7). He advises slaves to obtain their freedom and those who are free not to return to slavery, because they will have more freedom to serve Christ (1 Cor. 7:21). Don learned that it was an important part of spiritual growth to understand himself and the way God designed him, and then maximize his service based on that design. The two men read Psalm 139:14–16:

> *I praise you because I am fearfully and wonderfully made;*
> *your works are wonderful,*
> *I know that full well.*
> *My frame was not hidden from you*
> *when I was made in the secret place.*
> *When I was woven together in the depths of the earth,*
> *your eyes saw my unformed body.*
> *All the days ordained for me*
> *were written in your book*
> *before one of them came to be.*

Don's pastor challenged him to discover the unique ways in which God had designed him: his motivations, abilities, vision, style of working. To do this, they came up with a three-point program. First, the pastor asked Don to read a book to help him discover his gifts, abilities, and motivations. He recommended *Finding a Job You Can Love* (Mattson, Miller 1982). He believed that this book was one of the best to help Christians discover their God-given design, yet depend on God more than their abilities. They read a sample passage together (Mattson, Miller 1982, 41):

> The incompetency we see everywhere is not because people lack gifts, but because they are not in the right place for their gifts. They are not being stewards of what God has given them. There are plenty of gifts to do all the work that needs to be done everywhere and to do all of it gloriously well—so well, in fact, that people would go rejoicing from day to day over how

much was accomplished and how well it was accomplished. But the world's systems, corrupted by the sin of man, place enormous obstacles in the way of each person who attempts to find his rightful place in creation. Such systems assume that people and creation are mere fodder for their intentions.

Over the next week Don read the book thoroughly. It helped identify five key elements of his design: (1) What is Don most motivated to accomplish? (2) What abilities and skills does Don bring to bear in the accomplishment of that goal or goals? (3) What subject matter is he motivated to work with? (4) How is he motivated to work with people? Does he function best in the capacity of team member, individualist, team leader, coordinator, director, manager, or coach (Mattson, Miller 1982, 77)? (5) Finally, what circumstances or conditions trigger or foster his "springing to life"?

Don did the exercises in the book designed to reveal his motivational patterns. Even though he was a little doubtful about the accuracy of the results, Don was deeply encouraged that God provides ways for us to know ourselves, and that he approved of the process. Don was confident that at least he had made a start using Miller and Mattson's system. It did what all good systems must do: it provided some categories for a sober self-assessment.

The results showed the following: (1) Don was motivated most deeply to "improve, fix or make better." When he carefully looked over previous achievements that meant the most to him, Don realized that he was either fixing or making something better. Don remembered, for example, one of his first jobs, working in the college dining hall. He got so absorbed in the challenge of finding a way to make his job faster and easier that he got distracted from his work. (2) To achieve those goals, he usually employed his abilities to teach, communicate, and synthesize diverse information. (3) Don also discovered that even though he worked with others as a manager, he could also operate in the individualist mode quite easily. He was sometimes not sure which was most basic. (4) His motivations seem to be triggered in circumstances where there is something important to fix and he is sought out for help and given the freedom to carry out a solution. He remembered a water emergency in 1995 in which water engineers were given authority to resolve a severe drought in his state. This was a deeply satisfying assignment. (5) Don sought to understand what subject matter motivated him. He liked structures, but also liked systems and policies/strategies. Don carefully wrote up these results and, as he had other insights, he enhanced his descriptions of his inward motivations.

The Counsel of Friends

Don's pastor recommended that he continue his quest for information by speaking to his wife and to three long-time friends. Don asked them for their observations on his strengths and motivations. He also asked them about situations where they had observed weaknesses and lack of motivation. They met together one Saturday morning for breakfast and pooled their ideas.

Bill remembered the way Don had organized and led the men's retreat at church some five years earlier. He had to admit there were a few glitches (like the fact that no one remembered to bring the coffee) but the fellowship, the facilities, and the spiritual growth had been great.

Bill still remembered the night ten days before the retreat when the committee met and realized that only nine men had signed up. It was Don who stepped forward to encourage the group not to give up but to develop more direct personal ways of enlisting men for the weekend. Some twenty-five attended, and the conference had prospered since. Don also looked back on that retreat as one of the most satisfying experiences of his adult life. They all decided that Don liked solving problems and overcoming obstacles to achieve goals.

That "victory" was very sweet to Don. They also noticed that Don usually came up with systematic solutions. It was Don's idea to write the name of every man in the church on three-by-five cards and divide the cards among the committee for phone calls. This system was used each year, and upgraded with a computer database providing all kinds of information for the committee on the three-by-five cards. Don confessed that he actually found it hard to make the phone calls, but he did them each year out of loyalty to the goal. Others agreed that Don was more of a behind-the-scenes person.

Don's pastor pointed out to him that looking at the way one functions within the body of Christ can be very revealing of true giftedness. While the diversity of opportunities in some churches is limited, the advantage is that such roles are usually volunteer positions. Within your church community, you do what you are motivated to do, without the "warping" power of a paycheck and the need for a job. In the working world, those forces are used to mold us into what the corporation may want or need. That is not always what we are best designed to do. In fact, a 1976 study demonstrated that 80 percent of American workers were not suited to the job they had been assigned or agreed to do (Mattson, Miller 1982, 55). In contrast, the church not only exists without the warping power of money, but is richly gifted in the Holy Spirit with wisdom and discernment to recognize and nurture the gifts of God.

At this point, Glenda shared a revealing incident. She remembered the time about four years earlier when Don believed that their daughter had received a wrong diagnosis from their family doctor. The doctor had attributed some joint discomfort over a four-week period to "growing pains." When Don heard about the diagnosis that evening, he was shocked at the lack of testing. Not knowing how to confront the doctor, Don called a pediatrician, and asked whether such symptoms warranted more testing. The second doctor said it was a "judgment call." Glenda remembers how frustrated Don was with such an inexact answer. The pediatrician did at least give him a list of tests that could be performed. Glenda remembers it well because Don asked her to call the family doctor and ask for the tests, since Don was "busy" at work. Their doctor was a little irritated but ordered the tests. They all came back negative—after Don and Glenda paid almost $500 for them.

Glenda learned two things about Don from that incident, which she shared with the group. (1) Don likes to do things right, and (2) he does not like direct confrontation to achieve his goals, if there is somebody else on the team to do it.

Others shared stories that shed light on how Don tends to operate. At the end of the meeting, the group began to discuss the sales positions that had been offered to Don. While sales provided plenty of challenge, most positions were pure commission jobs. The group (to Glenda's relief) encouraged Don not to take them. They agreed, however, that he should not keep beating himself up on his engineering job. The three friends and Glenda now agreed that he should continue to look for another position. They prayed that God would give him grace to be obedient and faithful in his current job until God provided something else.

At first, the meeting with the three friends had been very scary for Glenda because she was not sure what they would say. But after the meeting she experienced a deep joy that God had given Don such faithful brothers in Christ. She believed that they cared about both of them and she looked forward to the comfort and fruit of their prayers. This strengthened her to go to Don and make an amazing statement. She told him that she was prepared for him to leave engineering for some new career, just as long as he was sure he would be happy in the new situation.

Researching the Job Market

The third big area that Don and his pastor agreed should be investigated was the job and career market. Don needed accurate, up-to-date information on jobs and careers that would allow his personal design to flourish. Don purchased a daily newspaper and found a lot of opportunities for those with specialized scientific or computer knowledge (which he did not possess), a number of engineering positions (which he rejected), many pure sales jobs (which he and Glenda feared), and executive positions for those with substantial management experience. Further complicating his search was the fact that he could not consider entry level positions since he needed to make $50,000.

Don did not find even one position that paid enough and for which he was qualified. He felt a wave of depression. "This is not going to be easy," he told himself. "No wonder I took so long to make this move." He suddenly had more sympathy for Glenda and his parents and their initial irritation that he could not be content in his engineering job.

About that time Bill called. Bill worked for the local newspaper and called to say that the weekend edition would feature an article listing the top hundred publicly held companies in their region. Bill thought it might help Don find out who was hiring. Don got the paper and · identified fifteen companies that were growing more than 10 percent per year. Bill also suggested that Don get information on those companies from his stockbroker. His broker gave him full-page printouts on each company and added seven smaller public companies that were expanding rapidly in their region. Most of them were high-tech companies, but Don was encouraged that he at least found companies that were expanding. Don called all the companies and ordered their annual reports. He read them to further familiarize himself with these growing firms.

Some of the businesses that interested him were in banking, securities, and technical sales. Bill had also asked Don if he had ever considered entering full-time ministry. Don asked his pastor and friends if they knew of someone in any of these fields. Obviously, Don's pastor volunteered to speak with him about the ministry. He also knew someone on the Christian school board who was branch manager for a bank, and Don did an informational interview with him. He discovered that this manager had gotten his MBA degree, worked for fifty to fifty-five hours a week, and was under a lot of pressure to sell consumer loans (home equity loans, car loans, etc.). He'd gotten his start selling real estate loans in the mortgage lending department of the bank.

Don also interviewed his broker about the securities business. He discovered that it was very individualistic, competitive, and sales-oriented. While you were in some sense your own boss, the firms applied pressure if you were not producing enough sales. If that did not work, they got rid of you. The freedom to sink or swim appealed to Don, as did the relative flexibility of the schedule. Earnings ranged from $50,000 well up into six figures.

It was tougher to find someone in technical sales. His neighbor's father-in-law, however, turned out to be just right. He was a former engineer who now sold heavy construction machinery (cranes, bulldozers, trailers, etc.) for a local dealership. Don interviewed him and actually accompanied him on a few sales calls. Don enjoyed the hands-on exposure to the work. However, he discovered that the salesman went to the office only when he made a sale, which was about once a week. The rest of the time he drove around by himself and heard people say "no" all day. He made $60,000 in an average year but it was a pure commission job. Don learned that this salesman got into the work when he was laid off from his engineering job and a long-time friend in the business had invited him in. Don found out that he was qualified for the work but that he might have to wait for an upturn in the construction business to have much of a chance of financial success.

He also interviewed his pastor to gain information on ministry as a career. Don had really enjoyed teaching Sunday school and spearheading the men's retreat planning team. The pastor pointed out to Don that he would have to go to seminary and so would need about $100,000 for tuition and living expenses during the three years of training. Don also found out the prominent place that "behind the scenes" personal ministry plays in the pastorate: personal discipling, conflict resolution, counseling, the enlistment of volunteers and officers, and personal nurturing of leadership. There was much more involved than the public teaching and preaching and the leadership of the church board.

Don asked about the impact of pastoral ministry on personal and family life. He was particularly concerned about how church-related stress might affect Glenda. The pastor shared some of his greatest ministry joys (hearing teenagers profess Christ publicly), as well as some of its burdensome aspects, like counseling people who are not open to change. All in all, Don got a good inside picture of the ministry—at least in his church.

While we cannot go into all the interesting details of Don's search for information, this at least is a taste of the kinds of information he sought and found. Don learned about the process and principles of finding a job, he learned about himself, and he learned about the situation. In short, he studied (1) the principles (the book), (2) the person (himself), and (3) the situation (the job market). Those three perspectives guided his information gathering. He needed to be sure that he understood the principles that apply, the people involved, and the circumstances involved. Now Don was ready to move on to the next step.

For Review and Reflection

1. How is the role that "the situation" plays in wisdom decisions different from the role "the situation" plays in decisions governed by biblical prohibitions?

2. How would you answer someone who said, "Gathering information on a situation shows a lack of faith in God's guidance"?

3. What are some other decisions that require gathering information before they can be made?

4. Have you ever tried to make a decision without the right information? Describe the experience.

5. What are the three types of knowledge needed for decision making?

6. Illustrate those three kinds of knowledge as they are needed in a decision you have faced or are facing now.

SUPPLICATION

IN Scripture, the Holy Spirit makes it abundantly clear that we are invited to call upon God for guidance. Here are some examples from the Psalms.

> *Lead me O, LORD, in your righteousness*
>   *because of my enemies—*
>   *make straight your way before me. (Ps. 5:8)*

> *Guide me in your truth and teach me,*
>   *for you are God my Savior,*
>   *and my hope is in you all day long. (Ps. 25:5)*

> *Since you are my rock and my fortress,*
>   *for the sake of your name lead and guide me. (Ps. 31:3)*

We have also studied the prayers of Paul, in which he prays for the church to have a knowledge of God's will.

> *And this is my prayer: that your love may abound more and more in knowledge and depth of insight, so that you may be able*

to discern what is best and may be pure and blameless until the day of Christ. (Phil. 1:9–10)

For this reason, since the day we heard about you, we have not stopped praying for you and asking God to fill you with the knowledge of his will through all spiritual wisdom and understanding. (Col. 1:9–10)

And, of course, there is the well-known passage in James 1:5, which we discussed in chapter 5.

If any of you lacks wisdom, he should ask God, who gives generously to all without finding fault, and it will be given to him.

If God promises to guide us and guidance comes by way of wisdom, which in turn comes by prayer, then prayer is central to the guidance process. A similar logic gives the same result: guidance comes from wisdom, wisdom is the result of the divine illumination of the Holy Spirit, and the Holy Spirit is given to those who ask. Therefore pray. Jesus says, "If you then, though you are evil, know how to give good gifts to your children, how much more will your Father in heaven give the Holy Spirit to those who ask him!" (Luke 11:13).

We also looked at how Jesus himself prayed to his Father all night prior to choosing his twelve apostles (Luke 6:12–16). As the "gospel blues" song reminds us, "If Jesus had to pray, what about me?" (Rookmaker circa 1976). Jesus is our great example and teacher in prayer. As you follow Christ, you are going to find yourself on your knees as you seek direction for your life and service.

There can be no doubt, then, that prayer is given to us by God as the means to obtain guidance. This follows naturally from steps one and two. In step one (consecration), we give our selves and our world to

God. In step two (information) we ascertain our situation in the world, and in step three (prayer) we offer that situation to God for his leading and guidance. He has promised to do that for those who seek it. He has promised to hear our prayer and answer it, giving us divine illumination in the ability to join the situation, the people, and the principles together in the will of God.

The answer to our prayers is obviously the primary benefit. But there are other things God accomplishes in us when we pray for guidance. One of these is perspective. When we spend time in God's presence and wait before the Lord for insight, we focus on who he is. We see ourselves, our situations, our decisions, our priorities in the light shed by God's own character and presence. As we do that, we see them in the light of eternity and eternal values. Paul says, "We fix our eyes not on what is seen, but on what is unseen. For what is seen is temporary, but what is unseen is eternal" (2 Cor. 4:18). My experience has been that the very act of meditating over my decisions in God's presence has had a profound effect on my evaluation of the alternatives. Sometimes a great idea winds up looking like a big waste of time when I am reminded of eternal values. It is in prayer that we specifically fix our mind on the unseen and the eternal. Prayer gives perspective, like looking down on a town from an airplane. The really important features stand out, the unimportant fade away. We have just a bit of the objectivity of God.

It sometimes seems that God chooses the occasion of prayer to put ideas and connections in our head. Perhaps he does it just then to help us learn that insight is a gift from him. Satan doubtless tries to take advantage of that phenomenon by inserting *his* thoughts as we pray. If, however, we put everything through the test of God's wisdom, we will be free to follow up on leads, thoughts, and impressions that come to us in prayer without being duped by Satan's tactics.

Additionally, I find that I am often much more creative when I am consciously bringing my decisions before God. God's involvement tends to blow away parochial barriers my fears may erect.

Another principle in prayer for guidance comes from Luke 18:1: "Then Jesus told his disciples a parable to show them that they should always pray and not give up." Persistence in prayer is particularly important in the prayer for wisdom because guidance involves the gaining of understanding. While messages from God, like e-mail, could be relayed instantaneously, God's method in guidance is wisdom. That cannot always be instantaneous. Perseverance in prayer is often required so that our thinking might be molded as part of our growth in grace.

I mentioned earlier that when I sought God's will about my ministry direction, I asked some close friends to guide me, as did Don in our example. Yet I prayed for another year after our meeting before it became clear. The insight did come in a flash, but it was a long time in the making.

Since God honors perseverance in prayer, do not give up praying. "Pray without ceasing" (1 Thess. 5:17). That means, do not accept less than the real guidance you need from God. He has said we are to pray for wisdom; to quit is to give up—not on yourself, but on God. The way you pray for guidance forces you to decide if God is just a vending machine to give you what you want within your time frame, or whether you are God's servant, seeking to do his will within *his* time frame. One of the greatest strengths of the wisdom view of guidance is that it encourages patience and perseverance in prayer because wisdom and insight do not come on command.

Such perseverance in prayer exercises and builds our faith from day to day. In fact, as John Calvin taught so well, prayer is the primary way we exercise (or express) our faith in the God of the Bible. We walk by faith, not by sight, and the prayer for guidance is one way that faith gets tested and built by the Holy Spirit. Do we cut and run when we can't see the way? Do we rely on control, manipulation, or escape to secure our future? All these express the wisdom that is from below, from our enemy. There seems to be little neutral ground here. With all that in mind, let's rejoin Don and his efforts to seek guidance through prayer.

Don and Prayer

After meeting with his friends, Don and Glenda decided to pray each Sunday night for wisdom and guidance about a new job for Don. They would set aside an hour from 9:00 until 10:00, after the children were in bed. This would give them time to update each other, share thoughts from the week, and pray for all the many intertwined issues like future stability, money, work hours, and moving. Glenda's wit and wry humor combined with Don's fear-induced rigidity to make for a comical but constructive conversation.

The first night, they got so involved that they talked and prayed until 10:30 P.M. Don's new consecration and Glenda's willingness to trust God had renewed their prayer life. They sensed God's presence and involvement and looked forward each week to this time.

Meanwhile, Don had asked Bill, one of his three friends, to meet him for a weekly lunch to hold him accountable for doing his present work for God's glory. They prayed that Don would not hide from responsibility and that he would face the tedium of his engineering calculations without underlying hostility to all around him. Don also used the time to run job ideas by Bill, to seek his help in crafting a résumé, and to focus his job search.

Bill also prayed regularly for Don, interceding for him based on the week-to-week challenges. In addition, Don gave his pastor permission to share with the church the need for prayer regarding his job.

Don committed himself to praying each day for insight into the important issues in his decision. He particularly asked God to help him assess the impact of this decision on Glenda and their children. She was not comfortable with high degrees of risk. Don knew that Glenda, after adding some humorous comments, would show commitment (within reason) to any scheme he proposed. Therefore, he knew he must take the leadership for any decision or risk exploiting her loyalty. He was convicted that he must look for a situation where she could continue to flourish, not just survive.

Don had always been very disciplined in his devotional life and so rose to the challenge of regular prayer very easily. Yet Don struggled with the faith that must motivate prayer. Don had lived in fear for so long that it was difficult for him to believe that God was really going to lead him. His prayers were mostly motivated by fear that God would not answer, so he prayed very consistently. Don thought that if he were still stuck in one year, he did not want it to be "his fault." He asked Bill and Glenda particularly to pray that, after so many years of avoiding this issue, he would enter boldly into the "land of giants."

Don was comforted that Glenda and Bill were praying for him with stronger faith than he had. Even Glenda was eager to see what God would do. Don's pastor encouraged him to read the accounts of Moses and Joshua to remind himself that he served the same God. He encouraged Don to make notes about what those accounts revealed about the character of God. Don did that with his usual consistency and, as a result, was much more aware of how God's character limited the downside of any crisis. Don was now ready to begin sorting out the issues.

For Review and Reflection

1. Is there a particular Bible verse that stands out in your mind as an invitation to pray for guidance? Which one?

2. What are other benefits of praying for wisdom and guidance besides the answer to our prayers?

3. Why do you think Jesus spent the night in prayer before he chose the twelve apostles?

4. Can you think of situations when you earnestly sought guidance from God? Describe them.

5. Do you think God answered you? How?

6. Do you have a habit of asking God for wisdom before making important decisions? When did that habit begin? How did you learn to do that?

CHAPTER 15

CONSULTATION

DON has consecrated himself and his work life to God. He has begun actively gathering information about himself, the job market, and the principles of "job fit." He has a strong prayer base within his church community and family. Now, because the decision about his future is not yet clear to him, he should seek counsel from "the wise" before investing enormous amounts of energy and spiritual capital in the search for another job.

The book of Proverbs emphasizes the importance of listening to advice regarding important decisions. In fact, Proverbs is structured as a book of advice from a parent or a wise man to a son, daughter, or other young person (1:8, 10; 2:1; 3:1; etc.). The need to seek and listen to godly counsel is in some ways the only message of the book. Ignoring the advice of the wise is, conversely, the primary sin (1:22–27).

Those who seek advice and those who reject it are contrasted sharply. "The way of a fool seems right to him, but a wise man listens to advice" (12:15). "Pride only breeds quarrels, but wisdom is found in those who take advice" (13:10).

Proverbs consistently commends getting advice on decisions. "Plans fail for lack of counsel, but with many advisers they succeed" (15:22). "For lack of guidance a nation falls, but many advisers make victory sure" (11:14). "Make plans by seeking advice; if you wage war, obtain guidance" (20:18). "Listen to advice and accept instruction, and in the end you will be wise" (19:20).

The tradition of getting counsel continues in the New Testament church as Paul appoints multiple elders in every city. No one man is sufficient unto himself. Everyone needs others who can come alongside to exhort, rebuke, encourage, or counsel. Twelve apostles submitted to each other on all important decisions. We also have Paul's example when he went to Jerusalem to confirm the gospel he preached, even though he had been taught it directly from God (Gal. 2:1–10). When a dispute arose, the elders and apostles gathered in Jerusalem and sought counsel together under the Word of God (Acts 15:1–21). Paul tells the older women to teach the younger women (Titus 2:3). Peter tells the younger men to listen to and respect the older men (1 Peter 5:5).

Resistance to asking for advice is epidemic in our culture—especially among men. I do my part to maintain the cartoon caricature of the stereotypical male who is too proud to stop and ask directions when lost. I like to believe I am in control, especially if I think I am "responsible." If we resist admitting we are lost when it is obvious, how will we learn to admit when we really need help—on decisions that deeply affect many others?!

Thank God that we do have a teacher, the Holy Spirit—the Great Illuminator, who under the leadership of Christ disciples us in the wisdom from above. He is more than a match for the foolishness of our pride, when we're too proud to ask for help. He is more than equal to our unbelief when we're too scared to ask for help. God himself is "wonderful in counsel and magnificent in wisdom" (Isa. 28:29). Isaiah 11:2 pictures the Messiah in the following language:

> *The Spirit of the LORD will rest on him—*
> *the Spirit of wisdom and of understanding,*

the Spirit of counsel and of power,
the Spirit of knowledge and of the fear of the LORD.

Even the doctrine of the Trinity points to the three members of the Trinity taking counsel together regarding the creation of man (Gen. 1:26).

To be linked to God means that we take on his character as God works all things together for that purpose (Rom. 8:28–29). I have been very encouraged by the effect that Christ's work has had in the lives of many—even men! They have humbled themselves before God and now find it a lot easier (even a delight) to ask for help from their brothers and sisters in Christ. They begin to reflect the wisdom of those who one day will judge the world and all the angels (1 Cor. 6:2).

Each of us, whether male or female, should seek advice on important decisions. We need advice if we are confident of a decision because most foolish decisions are "clear" to the fool. We need advice on confusing decisions because we are not yet clear. Parents, teachers, employers, elders, pastors, grandparents, relatives, and friends are all candidates to offer good counsel if they are wise. This was what Don pursued in the counsel he sought.

Don Gets Advice

Don now had to begin to give meaning and direction to all the information he had gathered and prayed about. He decided to call another meeting of his three friends and Glenda, and this time he asked the pastor to come too. Don wanted these people to give him advice about the alternatives before him. He knew that there would be certain questions concerning Glenda's risk tolerance that would be better to discuss in another setting, without Glenda present. Questions like, "Why is Glenda so fearful about a commission sales job?" "Could she be convinced that the fear is mostly hers?" "Couldn't she learn to trust

God to provide—even if you were in commission sales?" Glenda would want Don to talk about this, but not in front of her, since she was easily embarrassed by that part of her personality. Don decided to save those issues for later and just focus on job fit.

The meeting began with dinner at Bill's home, with Don and Glenda ordering take-out Chinese food. Don and Glenda wanted to be away from their own home to help them concentrate without distraction, and to be free to think in new ways. Don and Glenda prepared with special prayer that day.

Don made copies of his written summary of his own motivational pattern. He also wrote descriptions of each of the four job alternatives that had surfaced so far, with pros and cons for each one. He had identified two that had captured his interest: banking and technical sales.

There was a time of prayer before the meal. Dinner was served and the work began. Each alternative was discussed in the light of Don's "motivated abilities." The problem was that while the jobs that seemed available (with the exception of the ministry) were more enterprising (sales type positions), his deepest motivational thrust seemed to be to improve or fix, not to persuade, exploit, or gain response. His friends advised him to continue looking for additional positions or career tracks besides those he had researched so far.

Don's five informal counselors took the information he gathered from his interviews and tried to evaluate each of the four directions he explored. They encouraged Don away from considering a pure sales position anywhere. Technical sales, it was true, allowed him to build on his engineering background, but would not tap into his central motivational thrust to fix or improve. If Don took such a position, he would be constantly tempted to try to solve the financial problems of his contractors, instead of searching for contractors who had the money to buy his products.

"Full-time ministry" was an intriguing option because of Don's deep commitment to Christ and his successful service in the church. Certainly a pastor or missionary tries to fix something broken and seeks to improve or make better the people and the work of God. However, Don's pastor pointed out that his methods of teaching and synthesizing were too information-oriented and not people-oriented. Don was a great investigator, who could master and coordinate vast amounts of information, but most ministry challenges do not have information-related solutions. Moreover, the interpersonal conflicts that arise in a people-oriented job would quickly overwhelm a man who prefers his wife to make the difficult phone calls. So, for the time being, this alternative was put on the back burner. Don's counselors agreed that the financial problems of entering the ministry were serious but they could be overcome if Don were truly called to the ministry.

Of the four employment options, banking seemed to offer the best alternative because it had a very diverse work force with executives needed for many different capacities. Don seemed to enjoy management, was a good communicator/teacher, was detail-oriented, and liked an environment where one had to prove oneself. This option sounded especially good compared to his present employment, where any effort to prove himself was considered disruptive or divisive.

Another positive feature of a bank career was financial security. Even a loan sales position is not a commission sales job, so it provides more financial stability. The question was this: Could banking allow Don to express his central motivation? The group had a discussion on whether a loan "officer" sells or serves. They decided to meet again in a month, after Don gathered more information on banking careers and positions. He agreed to look especially for situations where his most basic motivation could be tapped. The group closed in a time of prayer for Don and Glenda, remembering Don's need to stay engaged at his present job out of faith in Christ.

Don went back to his friend the bank branch manager and asked him about jobs leading to a management position. The friend referred him to the bank's human resources officer. Don did an informational interview with this person and asked about the feasibility of a career shift into a management track position. The personnel officer was a little discouraging, saying that Don would be competing with all the MBA students. That would require a return to school for an MBA, unless Don wanted to begin as a teller at $20,000 a year or as a loan sales person at $25,000. He could then work his way up, but it would take time.

To Don, this news seemed to indicate a closed door. He prayed as he drove home to tell Glenda, asking God to give him the faith to continue. He was so afraid of failing after getting all his closest friends involved and putting Glenda through so much. It really came home to him that he was trained as an engineer and that without offering that expertise, he had no specialized skill whatsoever to offer. He was genuinely discouraged but did not let on to anyone but Glenda that he felt that way.

That night in their church prayer meeting, the pastor asked Don if they could continue to pray for him and his job search. He, of course, agreed. During the time of congregational prayer a woman stood up and began praying for Don. Suddenly she began to pray in tongues. While lots of people in Don's church pray in tongues privately, they rarely do so in public. Don looked up to see that the pastor was a little unsure of what to do. He let her continue despite their policy that no uninterpreted tongues be offered in public worship. However, after a minute or so she stopped and said these words: "Don, the Lord has compassion on you as a Father to his son. Though you are cast down, he will bring you into a fruitful land and you will find peace. The Lord will bless the work of your hands; they will sustain you." She offered some praise and sat down. The pastor also prayed for Don.

Don felt shaken that this woman had publicly put her finger on his discouragement. "How did she know?" he asked himself. After the service he thanked her for the ministry. She said it just came to her as she was praying and hoped that it encouraged him. That night Don pondered the message. Could it have been a message particularly for him? He was very challenged by the bold declaration that he was a beloved son of almighty God. Why would the son of the King worry about his future? He thanked God for that reminder.

However, he continued to puzzle over the last part of the "prophecy." What was this "fruitful land"? Was he about to be offered a job that paid $100,000? Or was it a long-term promise of heaven? He wondered if the reference to the "labor of his hands sustaining him" was a directive to look away from a management job. Was God trying to tell him to work with his hands? That seemed contrary to his motivated abilities. Could he have been wrong about himself?

After some prayer and consultation, Don decided not to change course because of the woman's outpouring. God would have to convince him from the principles of his Word if he wanted Don to change his job direction. His pastor agreed that Don should expect God to give him different wisdom if he wanted him to change course.

The next morning Don resumed his search, encouraged by the reality of his position as the King's own son. The human resource officer at the bank had referred Don to the bank's loan fulfillment supervisor. This gentleman suggested that Don go into lending but that he focus on problem loan workouts. Every bank, he explained, has problem loans. These loans and mortgages are behind and could be declared delinquent, leading to foreclosure. Perhaps, he thought, Don would be able to get into that area where his desire to improve and fix would be central. He would also have a very clear measure of his success and an incentive to improve his performance. This idea intrigued Don, and so he got a referral to talk to such a "loan workout" person. Don learned that an MBA was required for an executive in such an operation, but that a loan sales person could function as an important part of the team and have an impact on the success of the effort. The executive did caution Don, however, that it might take a while to get into banking since the high number of bank mergers left banks with many experienced people from which to draw.

This is a sample of the kinds of advice Don got as he sought God's direction for the use of his design and gifts. Don also went to see a vocational counselor during that time, read more books on the topic of changing careers, and visited a local school offering a nighttime MBA degree. At this point, he began to move into the stage I call "meditation."

For Review and Reflection

1. Can you think of a Scripture passage indicating that the three persons of the Trinity—God the Father, God the Son, and God the Holy Spirit—discussed a decision?

2. What Old Testament king regularly sought advice from counselors before important decisions?

3. Give an example of a time when the apostles sought advice from each other on an important decision.

4. What are some barriers to the young seeking advice from older (elder) Christians?

5. Have you sought such advice? From whom? What was the outcome?

6. What decisions do you face today where consultation with wise individuals is appropriate?

7. What qualities should you look for in those you ask for advice? Can you think of any biblical guidelines for selecting such people?

8. Do you think non-Christians can ever function as advisors? Why or why not?

16

MEDITATION

AFTER the death of Moses, Joshua was called to lead the people of God. God spoke directly to Joshua, issuing his new marching orders and giving him specific spiritual counsel. He said, "Do not let this Book of the Law depart from your mouth; meditate on it day and night, so that you may be careful to do everything written in it. Then you will be prosperous and successful" (Josh. 1:8–9). God directed Joshua to "meditate" on the Word of God day and night.

To meditate means to ponder something or to turn it over in the mind. Meditation is to the Word of God as "chewing the cud" is to the food for a camel or ox. The word in Hebrew can also be translated as "mutter," as when a person constantly repeats something to himself. It can also be rendered as "mourn." When a person mourns, he continually responds to a central event (a loss), but he expresses it and thinks about it in many different ways. Even the repetitive chatter of birds is described by this word. Meditation, then, signifies focusing on or responding to a central concept or truth, reaching out from that to the world, and looping back to the concept again (Clowney 1978, 12).

God wants us to approach decisions thoughtfully, to turn them over in our minds, pondering the different ways God's will may impact the decision. Wisdom is given to those who seek it with all their heart. It is given to those who look for it as for buried treasure. It is granted to those who do the work of thinking and evaluating before the face of God.

Unlike Eastern mysticism, such meditation does not destroy or obliterate the meaning of the object or concept of meditation, it enhances it. As Clowney points out in his excellent book on Christian meditation, Psalm 119 is such a meditation. There, the object or concept is the law of the Lord (Clowney 1978). Each section of the psalm begins with God's law, loops out and picks up content related to it, and returns again to the subject. There is a section in the psalm for each letter in the Hebrew alphabet.

Wisdom and meditation are linked in Scripture. Clowney comments on this connection (Clowney 1978, 16–17):

> Meditation brings wisdom, and wisdom brings success, not necessarily in the estimate of men, but through the blessing of God. Our lives become fruitful and effective when we walk in wisdom. . . . God's blessing of wisdom is granted as we apply his Word to the situations of our lives. We grow in wisdom (Luke 2:40, 52).

> Unless we meditate on how God's Word applies to our situations *today*, we cannot walk in wisdom. The directive insights by which we walk before the Lord are insights gained in prayerful meditation. Meditation is not a way of escaping our sorrows and sufferings by sliding into euphoria. It is a way of viewing our problems in the light of Christ's care and love, so that we may "walk worthily of the Lord unto all pleasing" (Col. 1:9–10).

The wise man considers carefully how he lives (Eph. 5:17) and the foolish does not. God promises to bless the ones who consider their ways and the ones who ponder their relationship to God's will and values (Ps. 1:1–6). Wisdom contemplates the counsel of God for our manner of life, our goals, our strategies, our relationships. It evolves into praise, prayer, communion, love, and obedience.

In emergency situations, some decisions must be made quickly. Our preparation and meditation must be done in advance or not at all. Yet there is usually time for at least an adrenalin-induced prayer of "Lord, help!" Other situations (like the one Don faces) allow time for reflection over weeks or even years. The time for such meditation is provided by God's own providence and we must simply make the best use of what he provides.

Pitfalls

There are, however, some pitfalls in this endeavor. First, meditation should not be confused with *worrying*. I have often caught myself "worrying before the Lord." That happens when I spend my time turning over in my mind what could go wrong in the future. While God wants us to count the cost and anticipate problems, musing on problems can divert and paralyze us from the fruitful work of determining what is best in the Lord's sight. If we find ourselves thinking about disasters as if they had already occurred, we are way ahead of God. We need to remember that he has not told us the future (as we know the past) for our own good. Each day's evil is enough. Instead, repent and give the future back to God, acknowledging that he will care for you and work all things together for his purposes. Refocus your thoughts on the merits of the options you are considering.

Fantasizing is another deadly pitfall. Like worry, it seems to resemble meditation but is actually something very different. Fantasizing is simply the opposite of worrying! It connects us to the future by an uncritical absorption with success. We visualize the goal or outcome as a done deal. We soak our souls in the power of fulfilled desires. But that kind of desire cannot say, as James 4:15 commands us to say, "If it is the Lord's will, we will live and do this or that." One often says, "I can almost taste it." Contemplating the joys of marriage, financial success, security, influence, and so on are natural enough as part of our creaturely motivation. They are part of the natural desire for God's blessings in this age. However, when we are driven by those desires, and close our eyes to the difficulties, costs, tradeoffs, and potential losses of these blessings, we are blinded to reality.

I see this phenomenon every week in the counseling office with young couples who fantasize about the good feelings they are going to have when they are married. They do not want to consider solving problems because it might put a damper on the feelings that drive them! In another vein, I have seen scores of people become fools as they followed "business opportunities" that promised them imminent wealth. Napoleon Hill's pagan book *Think and Grow Rich* (and many like it) encourages such visualization and the worship of that fantasized image (Hill 1960).

Another pitfall in the meditation phase of decision making is *undue haste* and *carelessness*. Those tempted with haste are not struggling with worry or fantasy—they just do not like living with indecision. They try to make all decisions quickly, reacting to their immediate thoughts, perceptions, or feelings. This is a denial of the importance of meditation. We sometimes tell ourselves we are in touch with our instincts, our "gut feelings." In such cases, we often have an unspoken belief that our "gut" is an organ of revelation. We have come to trust our instincts to provide guidance for our lives. But while our gut can provide us with lots of valuable nonrational data, wisdom is the means by which God guides us, not gut feeling. Our immediate intuitions are indeed important, but to walk in wisdom requires that we hold out for understanding. We may, for instance, sense something wrong with a person's views and not know why. That is very important information, but instead of making a decision on the basis of that intuition alone, we should heed it as a good reason to seek further information and insight as to exactly what we sense.

The Scriptures are full of stories about people who made decisions hastily, based on gut feeling alone. Esau, for example, sold his spiritual inheritance for a large bowl of soup (Gen. 27). In the same way, Adam and Eve did not consult together or seek God's counsel when they made the most important decision of their lives. Instead, they allowed themselves to be guided by appearance and Satan's version of the situation. Perhaps haste was part of Satan's temptation strategy: surely, he would want them to hurry up and sin before God could come to discuss such satanic propositions with them. David's murderous plans for Nabal and Peter's resistance to Christ's plan to die in Jerusalem were also understandable but ungodly decisions made from gut feeling.

Sometimes instincts can be very godly, such as Rebekah's disgust at the influence of the Hittite women in her family (Gen. 28:1) or Peter's desire to come to Christ on the water (Matt. 14:22). But the point is that when God gives us opportunity to meditate and consider our path, we should take it.

Many (but not all) of the decisions we make to implement the positive commands in Scripture are ones we have some opportunity to consider carefully. Most of the situations in which people have traditionally sought to "know God's will" involve longer term decisions, decisions like whom I should marry, which job I should take, and where I should go to school. Thankfully, God usually grants time to make these decisions, and we should make full use of it.

Sometimes we get *stuck in the meditation and consideration stage* of a decision, going around and around with no progress toward a resolution. Usually, the reason is the lack of some crucial piece of information. How much meditation does it take, for example, to decide between two colleges if you have the catalog and information from only one? How long will you need to determine if there is a healthy atmosphere at a certain company if you have never spoken to anyone who works there? Of course, *no* amount of meditation will help! If God in his providence makes that information available, we need to apply ourselves to get it. Meditation cannot compensate for our failure to order the college catalog, or our fear to ask the company's permission to speak to a former employee.

Very often, obtaining information requires enormous personal energy and focus. I am often tempted to ask God to short-circuit the need for such work, but we should not count on his doing that. That is tempting God. It is like throwing yourself off a building and expecting God to catch you since he is "obligated" to take care of you. So if you are meditating in circles because you lack information, concentrate on obtaining it, and then seek to consider the issues carefully. Keep repeating the process until you have the direction you seek.

Remember that God, your Great Shepherd, is involved in the process himself, fulfilling his promises to provide you with guidance. Trust the clear direction of God as you meditate and carefully consider your life. Though you may be unwise in the eyes of the world and even in your own eyes, God will grant you understanding if you fear the Lord and seek it his way. This was Don's experience as he began the process of meditation.

Don Contemplates His Situation

In his meditation, Don had to determine which scriptural values intersect with his decision. Specifically, he needed to understand which parts of the decision were really guided by biblical values. Which were equally moral and good in terms of biblical values, and therefore just a matter of personal preference?

Don set aside some time on a Sunday afternoon and, after a season of prayer, began specific meditation on the answers he sought from the Lord. Don began by reviewing the list of important questions he was seeking to answer. Number one was: What exactly was wrong with his current job fit? He could now identify three things: (1) There was no incentive to be successful in a large bureaucratic organization funded by government. Incompetency was tolerated and excellence was not recognized. That was very demotivating to him. (2) He had already concluded that the lack of challenge, the boring detail work, and the repetitive assignments all created a serious clash with his temperament. He wanted an environment where there were serious problems to fix. Except for the water emergency a few years back, there had never been anything like that. (3) Because he was so unmotivated at his job, he was afraid of failure due to lack of effort. He knew that as a Christian he must work with all his heart, but that took enormous energy from him. He came home drained and exhausted. Continuing in this position was putting himself in the way of temptation, which he knew Christians should flee when possible.

As Don listed these job fit problems, he sensed a new personal conviction that he must leave, even if it involved substantial financial sacrifice. Two reasons seemed to stand out. First, he was currently putting himself in the way of severe temptation not to work with all his heart. That battle was draining his energies. Second, God had designed him in a certain way and, as far as possible, he should seek to serve his neighbor (clients, customers, and larger community) according to that design and those gifts. Quietly, he asked God to show him if there was anything he was missing. He recorded his thoughts in his Job Crisis Journal.

A vocational counselor had advised him to keep such a journal and record everything of significance about his job search. He encouraged Don to write down what he did each day regarding his job: whom he contacted, phone numbers, the outcome of the contacts, new thoughts and ideas, etc.

Don then turned to consider the strengths he could invest in the workplace. As he reviewed the results of the Motivated Abilities Pattern exercise, he became more convinced of their accuracy. At least part of the picture seemed to be clear: He was an individual who liked to work in a challenging environment, where there were incentives and recognition of excellence, where he could play a crucial role in the fixing or improvement of a structure or system. He wanted to be able to use these abilities to communicate, investigate, teach, and synthesize information.

Third, he needed to identify some growing industries where he could put his motivations and abilities to work. He reviewed his discussion with his consultation group and his friends in banking. Although he liked the banking idea initially, it did not seem feasible. How could he get an MBA? How could he live on $25,000 and go to school? Despite his enthusiasm, he quietly wrote it off as impossible. He was not, however, ready to say anything to the others about such a decision. It was too discouraging to talk about.

Don then began thinking in an entirely new direction. What about customer service in an engineering-related field? He could help people fix problems, he would not be in sales, people would come to him, he could develop a loyal base of appreciation among the customers, and he could make a more reasonable salary. All he had to do was gather some information on opportunities like this in the area. He decided to do some more information gathering.

Fourth, he thought about Glenda and what her needs were going to be. After some meditation on this, Don decided, "Glenda really wants me to take her support for a job change seriously, but I still think I have to hold out for about $50,000 in income. Both Glenda and I have grown up in a middle-class home, and are used to a reasonable middle-class life. Neither of us wants to move into the city to secure cheaper housing. Glenda is also very involved with the church and the women in her

Bible study. After all, her conversion to Christ actually came through the Bible study. No wonder these women are so important to her."

In light of that, Don tentatively decided to look for a job for one year in his immediate area. Then, if nothing happened, he would look elsewhere. Glenda agreed. Further, Don and Glenda decided that they would not accept any move that would land them in a location without a good church and school.

Don jotted down these thoughts in his journal and concluded his session with another time of prayer. He prayed particularly about the need for an adequate salary and for contacts within the customer relations department of an engineering-related enterprise. Don's next step was to gather significant new information, which he proceeded to do over the next few weeks. However, Don knew that generating leads was not enough. He needed to take definitive action before too long. The next chapter follows Don through the next phase of decision making.

For Review and Reflection

1. What is the difference between Christian meditation and the meditation of Eastern religions?

2. Give some biblical examples of people who made rash decisions.

3. What Scripture passages command a thoughtful and considered approach to the issues of life?

4. Do you like Don's idea of a "job crisis journal"? Would recording your thoughts in a journal during periods of meditation be helpful to you? Why or why not?

5. Do you think a Christian can grow in the ability to think through and meditate on decisions? If so, why?

6. Have you seen growth in your life in this area? If so, how?

17

DECISION

AS Ecclesiastes 3:1 reminds us, there is a time for everything under heaven. There is a time to worship, a time to gather information, a time to pray, a time to consult, a time to meditate—and there is also a time to decide. Sometimes God grants us abundant time to decide, sometimes only a split second. But the season of decision making is under God's control, and so when it comes, it comes by his plan. In decision making we follow in the steps of Christ's own growth as God transforms us into his image (Rom. 8:29). Luke 2:40 describes Jesus' growth up until age twelve: "And the child grew, and waxed strong in spirit, filled with wisdom; and the grace of God was upon him" (KJV). The King James Version rightly brings out the spiritual dimension of Jesus' strength. Luke speaks in a similar way of John the Baptist, who also grew strong in spirit as he lived in the desert (Luke 1:80).

Growth in wisdom is the divine model, not instantaneous change. Growth in discernment of God's will (Col. 1:9–10) is brought about in those "who by constant use have trained themselves to distinguish good from evil" (Heb. 5:14). This training of the moral senses is accomplished in part by the seasons of decision making that God requires us to accept. We are "forced" to make decisions about how to respond to problems in relationships, about our financial priorities, our limits, our time commitments at work, home, and church, our long-term goals, our calling to specific ministries, and the investment of our abilities at work.

Frequently, the time limits for these decisions require the development of real faith. We may sometimes "disagree" with God about whether he has provided enough information for us to make a good decision in the time available. There are times when we face monumental decisions yet lack certain critical pieces of information.

Military commanders face this challenge in battle. In the Civil War, for example, Robert E. Lee had to decide whether to attack the Union positions that were dug in on the high ground at Gettysburg. His top general (Longstreet) strongly advised him to retreat and dig in on high ground between Gettysburg and Washington, forcing the Union to attack instead. Jeb Stuart (his chief cavalry officer) was "lost" and so Lee did not know the size of the force he was facing. He did know that it was growing rapidly. Should he wait and get information from Stuart? Or should he attack now? Or should he conduct a tactical retreat as Longstreet urged him to do? Lee believed that the best army would win and that the Civil War should not be drawn out indefinitely, so he ordered the attack. But Lee went on to lose the battle of Gettysburg.

Viewed in retrospect, Longstreet was correct about the tactics. He understood that the strategic advantage belonged to the defending force because of the new weaponry available in the Civil War. Yet Lee's decision may have drawn on a higher wisdom. He believed that to win a war, one must actually fight it. He had been in defensive positions up to that point and had always won. But such defensive victories never stopped the Union from attacking again.

Lee knew he must precipitate a decisive battle that would decide the war (Shaara 1996, 488). More delay, in his mind, would just cost thousands of additional lives and allow the Union to use up the resources of the Confederate States. He wanted the war to be decided shortly, even if he might lose. The loss at Gettysburg in effect decided the war and hastened the end to the bloodiest conflict of that century. In that higher sense, Lee may have actually done the "wise" thing. God may have answered his prayers for help in ways that even went beyond his own understanding.

The point to this story is that Lee was forced to make a decision without vital information. He was obedient to his calling as commander of the Army of Northern Virginia and went ahead and made that hard decision when it was needed. His confidence in God's providence and his obedience to his calling were the foundation stones that enabled him to decide under the conditions God had given him.

As Christians we make decisions in a very different universe from our non-Christian neighbors. We make them as a *responsibility* of our calling from God (as parent, spouse, worker, and so on). God has entrusted time, talents, people, and opportunities to us, and he wants us to honor his desire to see those resources used for his purposes.

In Luke 19:11–27, Christ urges us not to delay or avoid decisions out of fear of being wrong. In the story, the man who received only one measure of gold hid it in the ground. He did not invest it for fear that he would lose it. This unfaithful servant excused himself by saying that he knew the master to be a "hard man," with a reputation for expecting impossible returns (see v. 20). The master condemns the fearful servant, reminding him that if he really feared him, he would have taken the risks necessary to pursue the master's purpose, a return on the investment. Instead, the servant sought his own protection.

Decisions expose us to the risk of being wrong, yet whenever we allow that to control our obedience, we serve self rather than God. Dallas Willard reminds us that, as Christians, we must resist the temptation to try to use guidance to secure a life without risk (Willard 1993, 226–27). On the contrary, God often requires us to exercise great courage in making difficult decisions. The believer decides, resting in the wisdom provided and the promise of God's providential, redeeming purpose.

Boldness and confidence should be a mark of godly decision making, "for God did not give us a spirit of timidity, but a spirit of power, of love and of self-discipline" (2 Tim. 1:7). Our confidence to make difficult decisions will never be based on a godlike knowledge of the situation or its outcome. Nor will it be based on our own competency. Rather it must be based on the conviction that we are under the providence of God and are pursuing his purposes for our lives. We are jars of clay, yet we are indwelt by the Holy One, to will and do of his good pleasure. Our decision making is part of his process.

Therefore, the world for a Christian decision maker is a very different place from what a non-Christian perceives. We have seen that it is a place of responsibility to God as stewards of all he has given. It is a place where we are called to make stewardship decisions that carry out his purposes.

This world is also a safe place for a Christian to make decisions because of the sovereign guardrail of God's providence. It is a mysterious control that not only protects what must be protected but works in every event for the inner transformation of his children into his image. There can be, therefore, both the fear of God and a deep peace and relaxation as we make the decisions required of us.

There is no merit in making difficult decisions just to have them made. When a decision is not clear and God has supplied additional time in which to make it, we must learn to wait patiently while we seek the crucial wisdom or information. That dynamic is rooted in our expectation that God will supply wisdom and direction as we seek him for it. We hope for clarity; we continue to seek insight until it is given. God can overrule the process, but our job is to hope in his provision.

Some time ago, I went through some soul-searching regarding the future direction of my ministry. I began asking the questions and did all the things that I could do to seek insight. But for three years, the answers did not come. Thankfully, I did not have to make the decision right away, so I waited. I continued to pray about it and contemplate the issues involved. About a year later, the answer came to me. God granted the insight into myself that I needed. I saw both the direction I should go and the way I should get there. Of course, these plans, like all of our plans, are subject to God's revision. The point is that my part in the process had been completed a full year before God gave me the answer. I had to wait that long before I could see the path I should go.

Given the character of our God, the complexity of human life, and the confusion caused by sin, we should not be surprised if real insight does not come overnight. We should never give up if things do not become clear to us after our first attempts at decision making. God desires us to pursue insight right up until the time when the decision must be made. The patient pursuit of the wisdom with which we may better love our neighbor and serve God is deeply right and honored by God.

James 1:5 also exhorts us not to write ourselves off if we have made some terrible decisions in the past. God promises wisdom generously to all who pursue it sincerely. James specifically says that God gives it to all who ask and that he does not find fault. It is a request he delights to honor throughout our lifetime. This was Don's hope as he entered the decision-making process.

Don's Decision

Don had reached the point where he had decided to look for a position in customer service. He had identified two area firms that were rapidly growing and had customer service departments. But even as he made these plans, he was wondering if he was not just hoping for the impossible, wasting huge amounts of time and energy, and dragging his wife, friends, and pastor through a long ordeal. He wondered why he should expect to find a great job when so many people around the world do not have *any* job, much less one that allows them to live in some degree of middle-class comfort.

The next morning during his Bible reading, Don asked God how long he should keep looking before he called off the search and went back to his engineering job. He was reading in Genesis 7–8 about the time Noah had to stay in the ark. He noticed that waters flooded the earth for 150 days and then receded for another 150 days. After 300 days the ark rested on solid ground. He thought to himself, "That is what I want to do—rest on some solid ground."

Don (a typical engineer) noted that it had been 240 days since he first determined he should leave his old job. He wondered if God was telling him that in 300 days he would rest on solid ground again, just like Noah. After all, it seemed weird to be reading about this right after praying for guidance about timing. Don then calculated the date for the 300th day. He was shocked to find that it came on his birthday. Don was flabbergasted! How could *that* happen by chance? Don now began to anticipate being at rest on his birthday in sixty short days. Don thanked God. To him this meant that he would give himself until his birthday to find a job. After that date, he concluded, he would have been floating long enough. He engaged his job search with new energy, thinking that it would be over in sixty days.

One of two firms Don had targeted was a heavy machinery dealership where he had earlier inquired about a technical sales position. Though he disliked the sales end of the business, he did gather a lot of information on the company, generated some contacts, and began to wonder if he could get a position as a service representative. The customer service reps were making in the low $40,000s and he calculated that he and Glenda could tighten their belts that much. Heavy machinery is sold with some significant warranties and the dealer must service those warranties for the manufacturer. Don was, of course, very familiar with what these machines did, but he worried about the fact that he did not know much about how they worked.

He called his first contact there and, through him, actually got an interview with the owner of the company. The owner spent forty-five minutes asking Don about himself, his goals, his experience. Don left with the promise that the owner would get back to him shortly.

Don also pursued a position with a construction company that remodeled old factories and warehouses into new uses, both commercial and industrial. He had seen their advertisement for an environmental engineer. Don was excited by the problem-solving aspect of this job, the incentive and recognition it offered, and the opportunity it afforded him to go into the environmental field. His job would involve dealing with the EPA and other government agencies to convince them that the firm's remediation plans were adequate. He was a little wary of the fact that he would still be an engineer, but at least it would be in a competitive, growing company. He gathered some information on the firm, went to see some of their renovations and came away somewhat excited. He sent them his résumé and a cover letter. Ten days later he called to follow up. He was told that they had fifty applications and that they would call him if interested. A few days later they called to say they were not interested, since Don lacked experience in this field.

The next day the heavy equipment firm called. They were going to offer Don a job and wanted to see him right away. Don was surprised at his apprehension. He began to relive all the questions he had pondered over the previous year. Should he really leave a secure job just because he was not suited for it temperamentally? What would he do if they made him an offer and he couldn't bring himself to accept it? He would certainly look foolish. He knew that if he went to this meeting and they met his terms, he was almost obligated to take it. Yet it still seemed as though he was making the same decision all over again.

The next day Don went to see the owner, who got right to the point. "Don, we like your background and attitude. We want you on our team here, but it is going to be impossible to start you out in customer service." The owner continued, "We would like you to be on our sales team, and to help you get started we will put you on an $800 per week draw against your commissions—which we expect to be in excess of $100,000 within two years." The owner repeated his evaluation that Don would be good in sales, despite Don's misgivings. Don had not expected this and was in a state of shock. He asked for a few days to consider the offer. The owner asked for an answer within forty-eight hours.

Don got home and called to ask his three friends for prayer. Two of his friends thought that maybe he should take the job. Maybe the owner was right and Don was a good salesman. Don thought of the "prophecy" at church that promised him a *fruitful* land—maybe in six figures. One friend was against it, since he believed that God had not designed Don for sales or engineering. Instead, he urged him to keep looking.

Much to Don's surprise, Glenda agreed with that friend. She did not want Don to make another move with no prospect that he could do what he really enjoyed. "Sure, it's more money," she said, "but money should not control our vocational calling. The will of God should do that—expressed in what he has equipped you to do best."

Each of his friends promised to pray for him. Don and Glenda prayed three times over the next forty-eight hours, asking God for wisdom. The words of Don's friend kept coming back to him. "Serve according to your gifts," he would always say. Don reread Romans 12:3–8. To be sure, we are commanded to serve according to our gifts. The list covered both supernatural gifts like prophecy and more natural gifts like leadership. Paul keeps repeating, "If your gift is _____ then use it." Don thought about the fact that God had designed him uniquely for a reason. He realized afresh the unique individuality with which he was created by God. He sensed a growing conviction that he should turn down the job and wait for something that he could, in good conscience, say was a good fit for his gifts. He prayed and thanked God for the help and conviction of the Holy Spirit. He then picked up the phone, called the president, and turned down the job. He told Glenda, his friends, his pastor, and they all agreed to keep asking God to lead him to the right job.

Don was in a daze for about a week after this emotional decision to turn down a $100,000 job. But he soon recovered and was back out on the beat! He looked at other leads, which by now were getting very few and far between. Weeks passed. In fact, Don began to get tense because his birthday was coming up, his supposed date of "rest." He had not told anyone about his private calculations concerning Noah's time in the ark. He knew it sounded strange, and he feared Glenda and his friends would tell him to forget such artificial deadlines. In his heart he knew such calculations were not biblically justified, but the coincidence was amazing and he felt he needed something to hang onto.

But now it was creating tension as the day approached. How could he announce to his family on his birthday that God wanted him to stay in engineering? How could he give up when so much had been invested and God had given such clear insight into the kind of role he had designed him to play? His birthday came and went and Don was quite dejected for a week afterwards. He worried that he had disobeyed by not giving up his job search. He felt as if he was going to go crazy with this thing unresolved. But he determined to trust God and move forward in faith—continuing to look for a job where he could serve according to his gifts.

At the end of that week, Don came home from work to find a strange message on the answering machine. It was John, the husband of the woman who had injured Glenda in the car accident a year before. He wanted Don to call him. Don had not spoken to John since the accident. He wondered if John wanted to dispute the amount of a re-fund Don had mailed to him about a week earlier. When Glenda's car had been hit, Don had rushed to the scene and met John there. Don had been impressed with him and liked him. John had even given Don money on the spot so he could get a rental car immediately.

Two weeks earlier, when Don had received a final check from his in-surance company, he'd noticed that it included a full reimbursement for the rental car. In effect, he owed John the money he had given, so Don had mailed him a check for the amount. Now he hoped that there would not be a dispute about the amount he had sent.

He dialed, and John answered. Don was relieved at John's happy de-meanor. John said he wanted to thank Don for his honesty in sending him the money after a full year. After they talked awhile, John said to Don, "By the way, I would love having a person like you work for me in the bank I manage." Don was floored, but at least he had the com-posure to ask him which bank. It was a major bank, and it turned out that John was the president. The wheels of Don's mind were racing. He took a deep breath and said, "That's amazing, because I am in the mid-dle of an attempted career change, and banking is a field I am very in-terested in. Frankly, I would love to discuss it with you." John did not hesitate in the least but invited Don down to his office later that week.

The upshot of the story is that after some evaluation, Don was of-fered a management track position in the bank's corporate office at a modest but liveable salary. Don explained the results of his self-assessment to John and his motivation to "fix, improve, or make bet-ter." John, in a half-humorous way, blurted out that there was so much to "fix" or "improve" in the bank that he could keep Don busy for a hundred years. John seemed quite excited about Don, and Don sensed a lot of commitment to work him into the company. Evidently, the in-cident of the returned money had had a profound effect on John.

Don agreed to begin his MBA (with some help from the bank) and work in a management track position for a year until his gifts and motivations could be harmonized with those of the bank. The job required a fifty-minute commute each day and that dampened enthusiasm somewhat. But Don and Glenda believed that this was an opportunity for Don to use his gifts more obediently. Don could almost feel the approval of God as he envisioned using the abilities God had so carefully granted him. As Don and Glenda considered the commuting, they also reminded themselves that they could eventually move closer to Don's job and commute farther to church. Within a week, Don accepted the job and with quiet joy gave notice to his old employer. There was great rejoicing among Don's and Glenda's friends, and prayers of thanksgiving were offered to God for honoring Don's ethical integrity.

Although Don's story has an unusual twist, with God's providence in obvious control, such incidents are not really extraordinary. Most of us have experienced the wonderful provision of God at some point in our lives, in addition to our salvation. If God's given wisdom is the right hand of guidance, God's providence is the left hand. These two hands of guidance protect and guide the sheep along the way to eternal life. Every once in a while God will let us see that left hand, in an extraordinary display of his providence.

Don's wisdom also played a pivotal role in the appearance of this final, unusual gift of a job. He had done the hard work of consecration, evaluation, prayer, consideration, consultation, and had simply lived his Christian life trusting in God. He had also resisted the temptation to take a job that did not fit him. He had avoided being sucked into the trap of letting circumstances (the 300-days plan) and prophecies (the fruitful land—$100,000) control his response to the situation. All of this contributed to God's blessing at the right time and in the right way. Don learned enormous lessons of faith in the shepherding care of God. The story, however, is not over. It continues in the next chapter.

For Review and Reflection

1. How can Christians draw comfort from the fact that God sovereignly controls the amount of time we have to make a decision?

2. Can you think of biblical passages about people who failed to make a required decision or procrastinated in making it?

3. Can you think of a Scripture passage or biblical example that gives hope to those who have made foolish decisions in the past?

4. Have you ever faced a decision deadline when you thought you still lacked important information? How did you handle it? What was the outcome?

5. What are some ways that Christians can be tempted to transfer responsibility to God or others for decisions God has called them to make?

EXPECTATION

WHEN we make decisions, we do it with expectations that *certain things* will happen. What expectations can we have as Christians of the choices we make? We have already seen that God's providence works everything (including our decisions) for good, to transform us more and more into his likeness (Rom. 8:28). We have also seen that he promises that as we seek wisdom (by which we follow his will), we will spiritually prosper (Col. 1:9–11). These processes are ongoing in our lives.

What, however, is the eternal outcome of decisions like the ones that Don made? What is the net effect of our lives (and the decisions we make) on eternity? We know that because of our justification in Christ, we cannot be condemned with the world. We shall at least be among those "righteous that are scarcely saved" (1 Peter 4:18 KJV). Even in the worst case scenario, we "will be saved, but only as one escaping through the flames" (1 Cor. 3:15).

First Corinthians 3:10–15 is interesting in that it seems to state clearly that there will be different amounts of fruit evident in eternity from different Christians.

> *By the grace God has given me, I laid a foundation as an expert builder, and someone else is building on it. But each one should*

be careful how he builds. For no one can lay any foundation other than the one already laid, which is Jesus Christ. If any man builds on this foundation using gold, silver, costly stones, wood, hay or straw, his work will be shown for what it is, because the Day will bring it to light. It will be revealed with fire, and the fire will test the quality of each man's work. If what he has built survives, he will receive his reward. If it is burned up, he will suffer loss; he himself will be saved, but only as one escaping through the flames.

Although this passage is speaking about those who teach the Word of God (builders), other passages (2 Tim. 6:17–19) seem to make this reward principle applicable to the service of all Christians. When the fire of the day of final judgment tries each one's work, those endeavors which lack "quality" will be "burned up." Those who have built with gold, silver, and precious stones will be more clearly revealed and will be rewarded. Yet Paul warns that those whose ministry distorts the truth and those who minister out of insincere motives (partisan spirit) may well be saved, but their labor and their reward will be lost.

The earthquakes that occurred in San Francisco provide an interesting parallel to illustrate Paul's teaching. After the San Francisco earthquake destroyed a double-decker highway, there was great interest in which structures survived intact and which (like the highway) were *supposed* to be earthquake-proof but in fact were damaged. The architects whose designs withstood the test were vindicated and those whose structures collapsed were humiliated. The humiliated ones could be glad they were alive, but their reputation and credibility were gone.

Perhaps Paul is warning us of something like that. One day, Paul teaches, all the decisions we make and the actions we take are going to be revealed for their true quality. Each one of the workers on God's building should be "careful how he builds." That is because, to the eyes of the people, the difference between good and bad workers is not immediately apparent. We must be careful about our own work and mindful of the blindness we are prone to in evaluating the work of others.

In 1 Corinthians 3:18–19 Paul continues his discussion of the "wisdom of God" and "the wisdom of the world." Putting confidence in men, boasting about our teachers, or finding our spiritual identity in a distinctive teaching sets us up for disappointment and loss on the Day of the Lord, if not before. In point of fact, many (but certainly not all) of today's doctrinal disputes are but thinly veiled turf wars where denominational power brokers spar for more territory rather than earnestly seek understanding and unity (Frame 1991, 49). The damage to the church has been massive from such party spirit. Paul urges the Corinthians not to fall prey to the wisdom of the world. He says,

> So then, no more boasting about men! All things are yours, whether Paul or Apollos or Cephas or the world or life or death or the present or the future—all are yours, and you are of Christ, and Christ is of God. (1 Cor. 3:22–23)

So let each of us build on the foundation, not bringing in extraneous teachings or boasting, but carefully examining our work to see that it is of Christ in every way.

This passage is a powerful warning about our tendency to "use" God's kingdom (and the decisions we make as kingdom members) to advance our own kingdom and agenda. We, too, often seek guidance and blessing from God so that we will not fail in our personal goals. We pray for a healthy marriage, a fruitful ministry, or a successful business—for our own sakes, not Christ's. God functions merely as a means to our ends. Others also function as aides to help us reach our goals. Love of God and our neighbors gets linked to an expectation of a return on the "investment" of time and love and energy. That is, of course, not real love at all, but a form of manipulation and attempted exploitation. It is the wisdom of this world (James 3:13–16) that seeks clever and creative ways of attaining our goals irrespective of God's priorities.

We should be deeply thankful that God offers us his wisdom and insight so that the outcome of our lives will not be summarized as those escaping from their burning homes. He offers to disciple us so that we will not be those who give their bodies to be burned but lack love (1 Cor. 13:1), or who *would have* visited the prisoner if they had known it was Christ (Matt. 25:31–46). God offers those who seek it this kind of growing knowledge of their own hearts.

In addition to this warning in 1 Corinthians 3, God also gives us an amazing promise for the final outcome of our lives. It is found in John 15:16–17:

> *You did not choose me, but I chose you and appointed you to go and bear fruit—fruit that will last. Then the Father will give you whatever you ask in my name. This is my command: Love each other.*

This promise is just as amazing as the one it follows in verse 15. This is the one we looked at in chapter 5, where Jesus promises the disciples that he will tell them everything he learned from his Father. Now, in verses 16–17, Jesus gives the disciples control over the kind of fruit they bear for eternity. Jesus reminds them that in his sovereign love, he has chosen them to go and bear fruit that will not decay and deteriorate, but will last forever. Let's take a closer look at what Jesus is promising.

John 15:16–17 is a summary and climax to the first fifteen verses of that chapter. In those verses Jesus uses the metaphor of the vine and the branches to explain his relationship to us. We reviewed most of that teaching in chapter 5. Notice, however, what Jesus says in verses 7–8:

If you remain in me and my words remain in you, ask whatever you wish, and it will be given you. This is to my Father's glory, that you bear much fruit, showing yourselves to be my disciples.

Paraphrasing, we might say, "To the extent that you are abiding in me and my words are controlling you, I will grant your requests." Of course, these requests and desires will reflect the will of God. Jesus goes on to make that point clear when he says that answering their prayers will bring glory to his Father—because they will bear much fruit. In other words, the prayers of the apostles will be requests for God's will and priorities. And so, in answering their prayers, God is fulfilling his own plan.

When our prayers reflect the mind of Christ, God's answers bring forth exactly the kind of fruit he wants. God gets his will done, and we get our will done. It is the ultimate "win-win" relationship. It is fruit that marks us out as children of God and reflects well on the Father. In fact, it displays his character as the source of all love (John 15:9).

Our prayers are directly related to the kind of fruit the Father works in us. For example, if our zeal is for unreached peoples and it is motivated by the love of Christ, God chooses to answer our particular prayers by bringing fruit in that area. If our compassion and vision are for unwed mothers, church planting, Muslim missions, economic assistance to the poor of the church, Christian schools and colleges, ministry to homosexuals, orphans, widows, prisoners, or prostitutes, God promises that our prayers will bring fruit in those areas—in his time and way.

We should not rule out areas closer to home. We can pray for God's will to be done on earth as it is in heaven in our ministry to our spouses, children, relatives, and coworkers. Loving and praying for our neighbor is honored by God through fruit that will last.

This kind of promise stands out to clever, pragmatic Westerners as either unrealistic or magical nonsense. It is neither. It will not be just a prayer of words, because there will be grace within us that drives us to reach out to those for whom God has burdened us. Our prayers will not be our attempts to manipulate God, but rather occasions for God's agenda to invade ours. His agenda is summarized again in verse 17: love one another.

Ruth's Story

As we have said, God's promise to *bear fruit in us* will be fulfilled in his time and in his way, but it will be fulfilled. The story of a southern woman named Ruth illustrates this point. Ruth was born in the late 1870s, was married, and was blessed with eight children. Seven survived to adulthood. Ruth had a spontaneous love for Christ that radiated out to everyone around her. Her husband was an able and devout Christian leader, but Ruth's expressive grace filled the atmosphere of their home. Ruth and her husband Charles also developed a great love for foreign missions and named their youngest son for a famous Scottish missionary.

Ruth's health, particularly her hearing, began to fail, and she was unable to hear clearly what was going on around her. The older children helped out with the younger, and somehow the children got raised. Yet each of the children was deeply affected by their mother's love for God's Word and the people of the world who needed to hear the gospel.

Their home was a center for missionaries to come and speak to those interested in the work of missions. The children sat through many meetings in their living room, where they heard stories, saw pictures, asked questions, and got to know many missionaries. At one point, Ruth with her husband's permission sold her engagement ring to help out a missionary in particular distress. Ruth also prayed much for missions as she lived in the quiet world of the hearing impaired. She prayed through a list of missionaries on a weekly basis and instilled in her seven children the importance of the Great Commission. She prayed and dreamed that many of her children would catch the vision and be missionaries.

Yet none of her own children seemed called to missions. Ruth was deeply happy when one daughter married a missionary, but after they arrived on the field, her daughter died of cancer while still in her twenties. Yet Ruth continued to pray for missions and work for them in her own way.

God was not finished answering Ruth's prayers. One of her sons and one of her daughters were enlisted to serve at a Bible college, training missionaries. They each served over thirty-five years, training young people for full-time Christian service. Three of her other sons went into business, but before long they were heavily involved in supporting missions directly through their businesses. One of them became the treasurer and a major supporter of the Bible school where his sister and brother served. Through the gifts of that family, a dorm was constructed on campus and named in honor of Ruth because of the inspiration she was to her children and, through them, to thousands of young people who now carry the gospel around the world to hundreds of thousands.

Ruth has now gone to be with the Lord. But imagine the thousands and tens of thousands who have been reached because God answered her prayers for missions. Her children played key roles in the training of thousands of missionaries. In the New Heavens and the New Earth, I speculate that it will take millennia for those directly impacted by Ruth's prayers to meet her. And when they do meet her, they will express what we can literally call "eternal thanks" to her for caring for them. In a way, Ruth's life bore little visible fruit except that she taught her children the gospel. Yet God used them to launch the gospel through thousands of missionaries around the world.

God's answer to your prayers for kingdom fruitfulness may not be answered in the time and manner you expect. It can be (and usually is) something quite different from what we would have planned. It may not be evident for a generation or more, but on the great Day of the Lord, it will be revealed to the glory of the Father. Never underestimate the fruit-bearing power of God! Do not become weary in the work of the Lord, Paul tells us in 1 Corinthians 15:58, "because you know that your labor in the Lord is not in vain."

What an incentive to "abide in Christ and let his Word abide in you"! In Christ you get a place in history—that is, the only history that will not be forgotten. In eternity those who have the least honor now will be granted the greater honor (1 Cor. 12:24). As you bring the rule of God into your life now, you will be overwhelmed with joy then, when you stand before your Lord on the last day and see the fruit borne to his praise. Much of it will be a surprise to you, but there it will be, "fruit that will last." It will be the answer to your prayers for the kingdom of God. It will be your ministry dreams fulfilled *through your life* to the honor and glory of Christ.

But, we must ask ourselves, do we *have* any kingdom dreams for God to fulfill? I wonder how many of us actually pray and serve with such a perspective on the meaning of our short lives. What do our lives demonstrate that we are asking God to do? What passion or vision has God put in your heart for the redemption of the world where you live? Where do you long to see the rule of Christ extended?

It might be right where you are as you work from the heart for his glory. He says you will be rewarded in glory for whatever work you do for him (Eph. 6:5–9). That includes your job as your most extensive "good work." It includes your ministry to your noncommunicative teenager, your aging parent, your stressed-out spouse. It is ministry to the poor, to prisoners, to women, to men, to students, to children, to the unborn. Begin right where you are and seek to bear fruit for God. Develop a love for the work of the Lord, and begin praying for it. You do not know what a holy fire you will kindle in the universe of God's rule. God delights to bring to nothing the powers that are so intimidating, by the powers that are not and the weak things of this world.

As we look one last time at the developments in Don's life under the providential care of God, we can even begin to see some of the fruit-bearing process.

What Happened to Don?

Don spent a year at the bank's corporate headquarters. John, his boss, had hopes for Don in sales and marketing. Those plans did not materialize, and Don was not motivated by that kind of work anyway. On top of that, the politics of the corporate office did not sit well with Don. He was a very straight shooter and could not abide the jockeying for position that seemed to characterize the up-and-coming executives.

After a year, Don was happily transferred out of corporate headquarters into a district loan office. His job was to get involved in bad loan situations and try to salvage as much as possible for the bank. Don was motivated by this assignment and worked hard at developing "workout" plans for his clients. He put a lot of energy into this work and, despite his inexperience, served the bank and the clients well.

Then his bank merged and his position was squeezed to include four additional duties. It "just so happened" that one of those duties was to check out the environmental risks for the bank when it took a lien on a property that might be polluted. Don had some background in this field and shone like the morning star at this part of the job. He did it so well that his other duties were phased out and he eventually became the environmental officer for the bank. He also completed his MBA and now has what looks like a bright career path ahead of him.

Don's wife, Glenda, still cannot work a full-time job because of her auto accident. They did, however, finally settle with the insurance company for a modest sum. Glenda began a tutoring service for children with learning problems, and this has helped balance the budget, as well as provide her an outlet for her gifts.

With Don's MBA completed and his gifts well utilized, he is having a real impact for good at the bank. He loves what he does. What's more, Don has also begun to function on a Christian school board in need of his financial skills and his motivation to "improve or make better." Don has decided to begin a personal campaign to raise funds for a high school guidance counselor so that other students will not make the mistakes he made. He also continues to develop his ministries in his local church. Even Don's countenance shows the thanksgiving he feels for God's guidance along the path.

Don is just one story. God's guidance is offered to every one of his children—they just need to seek it from him and be willing to accept it. No matter what your situation may be, attach yourself to the Great Shepherd, Jesus Christ, and one day you will be able to tell your story. You will be able to testify from your own experience that the promise of Isaiah 42:16 is true:

> *I will lead the blind by ways they have not known,*
> *along unfamiliar paths I will guide them;*
> *I will turn the darkness into light before them*
> *and make the rough places smooth.*
> *These are the things I will do;*
> *I will not forsake them.*

May God grant you the sense of his sure presence as he leads you in the paths you don't yet know. He will illumine them with the light of his direction as he guides you to your destiny in his eternal presence.

For Review and Reflection

1. What Scripture passage promises long-term (eternal) fruitfulness to Christians who abide in Christ? Do other passages make similar promises?

2. If you abide in Christ and his words abide in you, what kind of answers to prayer can you expect?

3. In what time frame can we expect to see the fruition of those prayers? (See Rev. 14:13.)

4. What results do you long for God to bring about in your life (a) through your prayers and (b) through your labors for him? Do your answers reflect a unified vision of your life?

5. How do you want God's reputation to be enhanced through the testimony of your life (1 Cor. 10:31)?

6. To what extent is your daily decision making oriented toward these goals? How can your daily decisions get closer to serving those goals?

7. What disappointments, reversals, and losses have you experienced in your personal goals? How does the expectation and hope of John 15:16–17 give you hope for the success of your life?

ASSESSING MY PRIORITIES WORKSHEET (THE AMP WORKSHEET)

Overcommitted?

Do you feel overcommitted? If so, are you really overcommitted or are you just disorganized—or, even worse, a little lazy? Others at church don't seem as stressed-out as you. Maybe it's not how much you are doing, but the commitments you've chosen. Are they really the ones you should be spending your time and energy on? If you have questions like these, maybe you can identify with Bill.

It was 7:45 on a Saturday morning. Bill lay there, paralyzed. Who was he going to displease today? His wife? His boss? His fellow deacons at the church? His kids?

Bill had no easy answers. He was a Christian now, and he knew that he could not just "cop out" on the callings God had given him as worker, husband, father, church member, an adult son, and Christian. He really did want to walk worthily of his calling and please his Savior.

He steeled his mind against the fantasies of the beautiful and productive lake where he used to fish every afternoon after work prior to his marriage six years ago. Bill was alarmed at the amount of jealousy he was feeling toward his unconverted fishing buddies. They were probably there now. . . .

That feeling scared him enough to make him roll quickly out of bed, get dressed, and prepare to spend another day hopelessly doing the impossible. He would try to live up to the commitments he thought were part of his Christian life.

I have met many people like Bill, and they need help. I know, because at times, I have been Bill myself. The AMP Worksheet is designed to help Christians become explicit about what they see as the "oughts" in their lives, and to compare those "oughts" with the time God has given them.

Living Under Priorities, Not Pressure

This inventory was developed to help Christians apply Paul's teaching in Ephesians 5:15–6:18. Paul is speaking to the issue of godly priorities and time use when he says, "Be very careful, then, how you live—not as unwise but as wise, making the most of every opportunity because the days are evil."

While it may seem that this passage just adds to the sense of commitment overload, it actually affords a very freeing way out of the time pressure cooker. We have already discussed the principles of the passage in chapter 6, under the heading "Time." Here is a very quick overview of the relevant principles.

1. Paul teaches that the development and exercise of biblical wisdom is the key to enabling Christians to deal with time use decisions.

2. The challenge is for Christians to "redeem" (KJV), buy up, or use the opportunities God has given them before his return.

3. This is especially important since the days are evil. We live in the period of history where the final battle with evil is occurring.

4. Paul pleads for believers to bring every aspect of their lives under the control of the Spirit. The alternative is to be controlled (filled) by another power—alcohol, or any other life-controlling force.

Applying the Principles

In Ephesians 5:18–6:18 Paul applies his teaching by identifying the core priorities in each major area of life. These core priorities are framed as positive commands, which are themselves applications of the great command to love God and love one another as he has loved us.

The areas Paul identifies are as follows:

> ➤ *Worship and fellowship (Eph. 5:19–20).* "Speak to one another with psalms, hymns and spiritual songs. Sing and make music in your heart to the Lord, always giving thanks to God the Father for everything, in the name of our Lord Jesus Christ."

> ➤ *Church functioning (v. 21).* "Submit to one another out of reverence for Christ."

> ➤ *Marriage (vv. 22–33).* "Each one of you also must love his wife as he loves himself, and the wife must respect her husband."

> ➤ *Duties of children (Eph. 6:1–3).* "Children obey your parents. . . ."

> ➤ *Parenting (v. 4).* "Fathers . . . bring up [your children] in the training and instruction of the Lord."

> ➤ *Employees (vv. 5–8).* "Slaves, obey your earthly masters. . . . serve wholeheartedly, as if you were serving the Lord. . . ."

> ➤ *Bosses (v. 9).* "Masters, treat your slaves in the same way. . . ."

> ➤ *Personal spiritual priorities (vv. 10–18).* "Finally, be strong in the Lord and in his mighty power. Put on the full armor of God. . . ."

Although Paul does not cover every area of life (political responsibility, Sabbath resting, etc.), he does identify the core values in these major areas.

Paul does not allow us to decide which of these areas of life should take priority over any other area. He does not say, for instance, that your marriage comes before work, or that worship comes before marriage, or that personal spiritual growth comes before child rearing. Nor does he use these core values as a list of responsibilities arranged in either descending or ascending order.

Biblically, we are not permitted to decide to which areas of life we will apply the commands of God. We may not prioritize *between* the commandments of God. Rather, we must identify the most important activities in each of the God-ordained areas of our life and service. In other words, Paul wants us to fulfill our first priorities in every area of our lives before we fulfill lesser priorities in any area. A first priority in any area would take precedence over a second or third priority in any area.

Looked at from the perspective of time use planning, we should make sure we have completed all our first priority activities in every area of our calling before we begin scheduling second priority activities. In the same way, second priorities should be fulfilled before we move on to third priorities. Let's illustrate how this way of thinking could help Bill.

Wisdom for Bill

Here are some steps that Bill could take, using the AMP Worksheet, to assess his feelings of over commitment and see if they reflect reality. If he finds that he is over committed, here are some ways he can help bring his life into conformity with God's priorities and will.

STEP 1. First, using a blank AMP Worksheet (see the end of this appendix) and a pencil with a good eraser, Bill lists every activity he believes he ought to be doing to please the Lord in every area of his life. Some people may be organized enough to keep a log of activities and times for a few days to help them be realistic. Below are the kinds of activities Bill thought about and listed. He used three major headings: (1) God, (2) God's people, and (3) God's work in the world.[1] Other ways of organizing the list can also be used, and this particular list is only a suggestion.

Focus on God

Preparation for public worship
Personal Bible study and meditation
Personal prayer and worship
Christian books, tapes, and TV programs
Spiritual retreats and conferences
Public worship (including transportation time)
Family worship
Worship and prayer with spouse
Small group worship and fellowship (including transportation time)
Sunday school class
Other

Focus on the People of God

Stewardship of self
    Sleep—minimum and optimum amount
    Eating, meal preparation, and clean-up
    Personal hygiene, dressing

1 Chuck Miller, Discipling Ministry Seminar, Self-published by Barnabas—A Ministry of Encouragement, P.O. Box 218, Highland, Calif. 92346, 1977.

Exercise

Relaxation, entertainment, TV, video, movies, Internet

Reading paper, magazines, mail, catalogs

Sports, hobbies

Family relationships

Spouse—minimum and optimum, talking, "going out," fun, helping

Children—reading, playing, talking, teaching, and discipline

Family activities—playing, talking, fun

Parents—mine

Parents—spouse's

Other relatives

Transporting family

Children's activities

Household work and service

Chores, housecleaning, cooking, laundry

Errands, banking, gas, auto care

Bill paying, taxes

Repairs and renovations

Friendships

Discipling friendships (include phone time)

Other Christian friendships (include phone time)

Dating (if not married; include phone time)

Ministry

Ministry responsibility in the church, include prep time

Other Christian organizations, schools, missions

Personal ministries—not organized

Focus on God's Work in the World

Job

Time required to do the basic job, lunch, and transportation

Job responsibilities or overtime beyond that required

Non-Christian friends—list names
Community and political service
    Political party
    Service clubs
    Diaconal help to those outside the church
    Volunteer jobs
    Social clubs
Evangelistic ministries and missions
    Within the church or denomination
    Parachurch ministries
    Personal ministries
Miscellaneous—categories that do not fit above

STEP 2. Beside each activity, Bill indicated the relative priority of that activity. He chose from four possible priorities: (1) An absolute, non-negotiable priority; (2) An important priority; (3) An activity that is good when possible; (4) An activity that is clearly optional.

STEP 3. Beside every activity, he wrote on the worksheet how much time he should devote to that activity in a four-week period (28 days). The AMP required Bill to add in 35 hours (5 percent) next to miscellaneous to allow for the general mess of life, opportunities that cannot be scheduled, the inefficiency of life, and the need for some margins in any life. Bill put in a number for each activity that allows enough time to do the activity as it should be done.

STEP 4. Bill added up the total hours required in a four-week period to fulfill all these activities. He then determined how much difference there is between his expectations and the 672 hours available in four weeks.

STEP 5. Bill's total was over 672 hours, so he went through to cut out activities that are "clearly optional." His total still exceeded 672 hours, so he cut out activities that were "good when possible." He was still over 672, so he started cutting out important activities, trying to harmonize with the 672 hours available.

STEP 6. The column on the right of the worksheet leaves room for notes regarding each activity and what action is needed to get information, talk to specific people, or make changes in your schedule. If Bill, for instance, finds it difficult to decide what to cut, he can go back though Paul's teaching in Ephesians 5:18–6:18 and meditate on the core priorities taught there. He could also enlist the help of his spouse, pastor, or friends. Very often these folks have unique and helpful perspectives on what is really important and what only appears to be. Sometimes we need help in letting go of less important activities. Perhaps we are getting something unhealthy out of the activity and need help breaking the pattern.

This exercise can help followers of Christ grow in discernment as they explore which activities are most important in each of the relationships they sustain. For example, many wives have a very different view of the priorities in God's command to husbands, "Husbands, love your wives." The same is true of God's word to wives, "The wife must respect her husband." Bosses sometimes have a different view of the proper priorities of an employee's work. The same can be true of parents to adult children, pastors to church members, and even friend to friend.

Underneath the drive to bring Bill's self-expectations (oughts) into line with the time God has allowed was the bedrock belief that God never gives us more than it is possible to do. That must empower our faith as we seek to discern the nonnegotiable from the important, the good, and the optional. Paul prays for the Philippians that their "love may abound more and more in knowledge and depth of insight, so that you may be able to discern what is best" (Phil. 1:9–10).

This discernment can be sought and developed so that we can accurately assess God's will in our priorities and schedules. It enables us to live in his will with greater integrity. It brings with it the fruit of greater peace (about not doing everything), greater confidence about what you choose to do, and a renewed motivation and joy to realize that the Christian life is not impossible to live.

When Bill first filled out his AMP Worksheet, his commitments added up to 875 hours. He was shocked that his expectations and God's expectations were 200 hours a month out of sync. Initially, he was 200 hours out of the will of God!

Bill ended up going to his wife and pastor and asking for help. They came back with suggestions for cuts and exchanges in the "Important" category. They recommended that Bill resign from two ministries in the church (Sunday school teaching and budget committee) but urged him to remain a deacon and focus on leading the financial counseling ministry within the church. The pastor even helped Bill make some phone calls to cancel commitments that he had unwisely made.

They honed Bill's priorities and hours until he had time to be home or with the family four nights a week. His wife had found herself increasingly exhausted from her part-time job when she also had to manage the home by herself in the evenings. They all agreed that he should have at least one of those nights to focus on in-depth communication and prayer with his wife. They also added one night a month for friendship with non-Christian friends and neighbors, and decided that half-day fishing trips are important for Bill every month or so. They also planned a fun night out for them as a couple every month—with dates set in advance to keep them from being crowded out by other commitments.

Bill's revised AMP (shown on pp. 272–73) still reflected some

Assessing My Priorities Worksheet

Activities — List All Your Activities	Relative Priority — Non-negotiable	Important	Good when possible	Clearly optional	Time — Hours required in 28 days	Changes Needed — How to make needed changes
Personal worship, devotions	x				4	
Family worship	x				4	
Small group fellowship	x				6	
Prayer with spouse	x				4	
Church and Sunday school class	x				12	
Sunday reading		x			4	
Sleep—minimum	x				196	
Sleep—additional			x		14	
Dress, wash, clothes	x				7	
Exercise		x			6	
Eating—breakfast, dinner	x				28	
Relax—TV, "A"		x			12	
Relax—TV, "B"			x		12	
Reading, paper		x			12	
Sports league		x			4	
House repair		x			4	
Bills, taxes, bank	x				4	

Activity				Hours
Weekly conference with spouse			x	8
Communication with spouse (daily)			x	14
Going "out"			x	3
Relaxing with spouse			x	14
Help with chores, shopping		x		14
Children—talking, reading			x	14
Kids sports		x		4
Family activities		x		12
Parents			x	8
Friends		x		4
Primary ministries			x	20
Secondary ministries		x		5
Rotary club		x		4
Job—basic			x	180
Job—extra time	x			20
Miscellaneous				35

Total Time Required	692
Time Provided	672
Difference	20

Activities		Relative Priority				Time	Changes Needed
List All Your Activities		Clearly optional	Good when possible	Important	Non-negotiable	Hours required in 28 days	How to make needed changes

																							Total Time Required	
																							Time Provided	
																							Difference	

twenty hours of illegitimate "oughts"—because he had either too many activities or too much time given to some of them. But at least now he was reasonably close to the 672-hour goal. He could now continue to refine his commitments to move toward 672 hours.

Bill was depressed for two weeks after the calls were made. He felt like some kind of traitor—particularly to the ministries he was quitting. But slowly he entered into his new priorities with much more motivation and creativity. He found his heart more engaged with these activities because he knew they were possible to do well and because he knew he was much closer to doing the will of God.

The AMP Worksheet can also be useful for those who appear to be under-challenged, unproductive, or wasteful of time. It can be the occasion for fruitful discussions of the rich scriptural teaching on the need to be stewards of our time and the need to avoid idleness or drift into priorities that focus on leisure, self-indulgence, riches, personal isolation, escape, and a host of other pitfalls. Whatever its use, I hope that it will be a practical help to Christians learning to live obediently by priorities and not pressure or self-oriented pleasure.

(The AMP Worksheet may be reproduced for private use and group discussion. Additional copies of this appendix can be obtained by calling Resources for Changing Lives at 1-800-318-2186.)

WORKS CITED

Adams, Jay. 1966. *Guidance in Counseling*. Michigan City, Ind.: Sound Word Associates, NANC Tape Library.

Clowney, Edmund. 1978. *CM*, Christian Meditation*. Nutley, N.J.: Craig Press.

———. 1995. *The Church*. Downers Grove, Ill.: InterVarsity Press.

Davis, John D. 1924. *Davis Dictionary of the Bible*. Grand Rapids: Baker.

The Economist, Staff writer. 1996. "Mobility in America; Up, Down and Standing Still." London: *The Economist*, February 24, 1996, 30–31.

Ellis, Peter B. 1994. *The Druids*. London: Constable and Company.

Ferguson, Sinclair. 1982. *Discovering God's Will*. Edinburgh: Banner of Truth.

Frame, John. 1991. *Evangelical Reunion*. Grand Rapids: Baker.

Friesen, Garry. 1980. *Decision Making and the Will of God*. Portland, Ore.: Multnomah Press.

Geiser, Kenneth. 1968. "If You Have Missed God's Best." In *Essays on Guidance,* edited by Joseph Bayly. Madison, Wis.: InterVarsity Press.

Gould, Stephen. 1996. *The Glorious Accident*. PBS Television Production of WHYY, Wilmington, Del.

Hicks, Robert. 1995. *In Search of Wisdom*. Colorado Springs: Nav-Press.

Hill, Napoleon. 1960. *Think and Grow Rich*. Greenwich, Conn.: Faucett.

Hodge, Charles. 1865. *Systematic Theology*. Grand Rapids: Eerdmans.

Maeder, Gary. 1973. *God's Will for Your Life*. Wheaton, Ill.: Tyndale House.

Mattson, Ralph, and Arthur Miller. 1982. *Finding a Job You Can Love*. Nashville, Tenn.: Nelson.

Meyer, F. B. 1896. *The Secret of Guidance*. New York: Fleming H. Revell Co.

Miller, Chuck. 1977. *Discipling Ministry Seminar*. Self-published by Barnabas—A Ministry of Encouragement, Highland, Calif.

Murray, John. 1965. *The Epistle to the Romans*. Vol. 1, The New International Commentary on the New Testament. Grand Rapids: Eerdmans.

Oosthuizen, G. C., S. D. Edwards, W. H. Wessels, I. Hexham, 1988. *Afro-Christian Religion and Healing in Southern Africa. African Studies, Volume 8*. Lampeter, Wales: The Edwin Mellen Press.

Rookmaker, Hans. (circa 1976). Selected private recordings of the Spirit of Memphis Quartet.

Ross, Hugh. 1991. *The Fingerprint of God*. Orange, Calif.: Promise.

Ryle, James. 1995. *A Dream Come True*. Lake Mary, Fla.: Creation House.

Sanders, J. Oswald. 1992. *Every Life a Plan of God*. Grand Rapids: Discovery House.

Schwab, George M. 1995. "The Proverbs and the Art of Persuasion." In *The Journal of Biblical Counseling*, edited by David Powlison, vol. 14, no. 1.

Shaara, Jeff. 1996. *Gods and Generals*. New York: Ballantine.

Sine, Tom. 1987. *Why Settle for More and Miss the Best*. Dallas, Tex.: Word.

Smith, M. Blaine. 1991. *Knowing God's Will.* Downers Grove, Ill.: InterVarsity Press.

Staton, Knofel. 1968. *How to Know the Will of God.* Cincinnati, Ohio: New Life, a division of Standard Publishing.

Van Til, Cornelius. (n.d.). *Survey of Christian Epistemology.* Philadelphia: Presbyterian and Reformed.

Waltke, Bruce. 1995. *Finding the Will of God.* Gresham, Ore.: Vision House.

Welch, Edward T. 1997. *When People Are Big and God Is Small.* Phillipsburg, N.J.: P&R Publishing.

The Westminster Confession of Faith, 1648. In *Trinity Hymnal.* Philadelphia: Orthodox Presbyterian Church, 1961.

Willard, Dallas. 1993. *In Search of Guidance.* New York: HarperCollins.

Winship, Michael. 1996. *The Seers of God.* Baltimore, Md.: Johns Hopkins University Press.

RESOURCES FOR CHANGING LIVES

Addictions—A Banquet in the Grave: Finding Hope in the Power of the Gospel.
Edward T. Welch shows how addictions result from a worship disorder—idolatry—and how they are overcome by the power of the gospel. 0-87552-606-3

Age of Opportunity: A Biblical Guide to Parenting Teens. Paul David Tripp
uncovers the heart issues affecting parents' relationship with their teenagers.
0-87552-605-5

*Blame It on the Brain? Distinguishing Chemical Imbalances, Brain Disorders, and
Disobedience.* Edward T. Welch compares the roles of the brain and the "heart" in
problems such as alcoholism, depression, ADD, and homosexuality. *0-87552-602-0*

Step by Step: Divine Guidance for Ordinary Christians. James C. Petty sifts
through approaches to knowing God's will and illustrates how to make biblically
wise decisions. *0-87552-603-9*

War of Words: Getting to the Heart of Your Communication Struggles. Paul David
Tripp takes us beyond superficial solutions in the struggle to control our tongues.
0-87552-604-7

*When People Are Big and God Is Small: Overcoming Peer Pressure, Co-
dependency, and the Fear of Man.* Edward T. Welch exposes the spiritual dimen-
sions of pride, defensiveness, people-pleasing, needing approval, "self-esteem," etc.
0-87552-600-4

Booklet Series: A.D.D; Anger; Depression; Domestic Abuse; Forgiveness; God's
Love; Homosexuality; "Just One More"; Marriage; Pornography; Pre-Engagement;
Priorities; Suffering; Teens and Sex; Thankfulness

FOR FURTHER INFORMATION

Speaking engagements with authors in this series may be arranged by calling The Christian
Counseling and Educational Foundation at (215) 884-7676.

Videotapes and audio cassettes by authors in this series may be ordered through Resources
for Changing Lives at (800) 318-2186.

For a complete catalog of titles from P&R Publishing, call (800) 631-0094.